Praise for

LEAD LAST

"Olaolu Ogunyemi flips the script on leadership. *Lead Last* shows us that real leaders don't chase the spotlight—they lift others, build trust, and lead with purpose. This book won't just sit on your shelf—it will change how you show up every day as a leader."

Dr. Marshall Goldsmith, Thinkers50 #1 executive coach and *New York Times* bestselling author of *The Earned Life*, *Triggers*, and *What Got You Here Won't Get You There*

"Olaolu challenges leaders to look inward and understand themselves and those they lead to become the kind of leader who empowers and inspires others. Through insightful, practical principles, Olaolu offers a no-nonsense road map to navigating today's ever-changing landscape of technology and evolving workplace norms while fostering a positive, productive work environment free from toxic culture and negativity."

Tommy Spaulding, *New York Times* bestselling author of *The Heart-Led Leader* and *The Gift of Influence*

"*Lead Last* is a great read chock-full of leadership gems just waiting to be mined!"

James C. Hunter, author of the international bestseller *The Servant*

"*Lead Last* is a refreshing and essential guide for anyone aspiring to make a genuine, lasting impact in their leadership journey. It moves beyond quick fixes, offering a practical road map for profound self-discovery and people-first leadership. It's like a self-help book, a leadership conference, and a pep rally all rolled into one!"

Todd Henry, author of *The Brave Habit*

"Brilliantly organized, straight to the point, and easy to comprehend . . . I recommend *Lead Last* to all leaders in business and other organizations. Anyone passionate about leadership will definitely appreciate this book."

Readers' Favorite

LEAD LAST

Twenty-One Counterintuitive Principles for Becoming an Effective Leader

OLAOLU OGUNYEMI

www.amplifypublishinggroup.com

Lead Last: Twenty-One Counterintuitive Principles for Becoming an Effective Leader

For more information, please contact:
Amplify Publishing, an imprint of Amplify Publishing Group
620 Herndon Parkway, Suite 220
Herndon, VA 20170
info@amplifypublishing.com

Library of Congress Control Number: 2025926990

CPSIA Code: PRV0126A

ISBN-13: 979-8-89138-971-7

Printed in the United States

I dedicate this book to my beautiful wife and children, who have made me a better man and taught me how to become an empathetic listener and an affectionate leader. I love you, and I am immensely proud of you!

My parents and siblings established a firm foundation and set the bar high for me. You continue to impress me with your love, accountability, gifts, and genuine care for me and my family.

My friends, mentors, and P2C family have created an encouraging community. You provide support, valuable advice, and wise guidance when I need it most.

The United States Marine Corps has continuously allowed me to lead and experience the joy and honor of serving in the Marines.

And my fellow Marines with whom I have had the pleasure of working—your patience, camaraderie, and warrior ethos have solidified my lifelong commitment to friendships and love for this "gun club" and what we do.

Semper fidelis!

CONTENTS

INTRODUCTION ix

PART 1: WHO ARE YOU?

PRINCIPLE #1
LET YOUR GUARD DOWN 9

PRINCIPLE #2
SHARE THE MOMENTS 15

PRINCIPLE #3
LEAD BY SHARING GOALS 21

PRINCIPLE #4
BE YOURSELF BUT ADAPT YOUR MANAGEMENT STYLE TO THE TEAM YOU HAVE 27

PRINCIPLE #5
BE STUDIOUS 33

PRINCIPLE #6
BE STABLE AND LEVEL-HEADED 37

PRINCIPLE #7
ORGANIZATION IS KEY 45

PART 2: WHO ARE YOU LEADING?

PRINCIPLE #8
EVERYONE'S BACKGROUND IS IMPORTANT 63

PRINCIPLE #9

CANCEL COMPLAINING 69

PRINCIPLE #10

IDENTIFY AND MEET EACH TEAM MEMBER'S NEEDS 75

PRINCIPLE #11

TRAINING DEFICIENCIES CAN BE REMEDIED; CHARACTER FLAWS CANNOT 83

PRINCIPLE #12

BUILD EACH OTHER UP 91

PRINCIPLE #13

GIVE YOUR TEAM MEMBERS A VOICE 101

PRINCIPLE #14

DIRECT FEEDBACK BEATS GOSSIPING EVERY TIME 105

PART 3: HOW ARE YOU LEADING? INFLUENCING THE CULTURE

PRINCIPLE #15

MEET PROBLEMS HEAD-ON 115

PRINCIPLE #16

HOLD THE LINE 121

PRINCIPLE #17

PREPARE THE NEXT GENERATION 129

PRINCIPLE #18

FOSTER CREATIVITY, INNOVATION, AND RESOURCEFULNESS 135

PRINCIPLE #19

DON'T BE LORD OF THE ~~FLIES~~ TASKS 143

PRINCIPLE #20

IT'S A WORKPLACE, NOT A LOCKER ROOM 151

PRINCIPLE #21

YOU'RE LEADING HUMANS *AND* "ROBOTS" 155

FINAL THOUGHT 163

EPILOGUE 165

APPENDIX

THE LASTING LEADERSHIP TOOLKIT 169

REFERENCES 179

MEET THE AUTHOR 183

INTRODUCTION

There I was, driving down the streets of Jacksonville, North Carolina, with my mind completely consumed by one question: "What do leaders truly need to succeed?" I was on a mission to create a book that wouldn't just sit on someone's shelf but would genuinely change how they lead. I needed something catchy and unique. That's when the perfect title hit me:

Lead Last.

The idea made me laugh and reflect—two signs of a title worth keeping. *Lead Last* is a spin-off of an old quote, a play on words, and maybe the result of me running in freezing temperatures that morning, causing my brain not to function as well. We'll assume the latter observation is not the case and home in on the first two.

The original quote is: "He who laughs last laughs best." My spin-off is:

He who leads last leads best!

Leadership isn't about being the first to act or grabbing attention. It's about learning, observing, and prioritizing others' needs over your own. I'm challenging the assertion that leaders are born with the traits and qualities they need to demonstrate effective leadership. People aren't *born* leaders; they are *learned* leaders.

This book argues that you should learn about yourself and who you are leading before becoming an effective leader. As Donald T. Phillips explains in *Lincoln on Leadership*, great leaders are shaped by life's lessons (Phillips 1992). Mentors, experiences, and intentional practice mold them. The lessons we learn throughout childhood and adulthood help us form the traits we need to be effective leaders.

The Impact of Your Leadership Lasts

True leadership creates ripples that extend beyond the immediate moment. Our leadership should permeate the entire organization and leave a legacy of growth, transformation, and purpose in the lives of those we lead. Our influence on others should leave an indelible mark on their lives—assuming they were receptive to our leadership. My goal is for you to use the practical advice in this book to refine your leadership abilities and become an inspirational leader capable of changing lives, improving your workplace culture, and efficiently accomplishing your organization's mission. This book is designed to help you learn more about yourself, examine and adapt to who you're leading, and become an effective leader.

So, What Is This Book *Really* About?

This book isn't about quick fixes or flashy gimmicks. It's a practical guide to developing the traits and skills that inspire trust, foster collaboration, and achieve lasting results. You'll explore how to understand yourself, connect deeply with those you lead, and leave a legacy that speaks louder than words. Applying what you learn in this book will make you a more effective leader.

Lead Last is divided into three parts, each with seven practical leadership principles:

- **Part 1: Who Are You?** This part will challenge you to take an introspective look at who you are and what your purpose is.
- **Part 2: Who Are You Leading?** I'm an advocate for people-first leadership, but how can you lead people if you don't know them? Don't worry, you'll learn more about the people you lead in this part.
- **Part 3: How Are You Leading? Influencing the Culture.** This is where you will learn how to create an environment that fosters innovative self-starters committed to accomplishing the mission.

At the end, you'll enjoy *The Lasting Leadership Toolkit* in the appendix. This appendix is a collection of tools, frameworks, and real-world case studies inspired by conversations with senior leaders and beta readers. Use this section to translate principles into practice as you face real leadership challenges, especially in areas where the principles appear to clash. Think of it as your personal field manual for applying what you've learned in *Lead Last* long after you close the final chapter.

Why Should *All* Leaders Read *Lead Last*?

Lead Last redefines leadership by challenging the notion that leaders must be in the spotlight to drive success. Instead, it empowers readers to lead from behind—putting others first, fostering authentic relationships, and creating a culture of trust and collaboration.

Whether you're taking your first steps as an emerging leader or you're a seasoned professional with ten to fifteen years under your belt seeking to refine your experience, *Lead Last* offers actionable insights rooted in real-world challenges for you. Unlike traditional leadership books, it offers counterintuitive, actionable principles rooted in humility and practicality, such as embracing a closed-door policy, challenging the usefulness of venting, leading "robots," and focusing on team synergy over individual accolades.

You will feel seen and inspired by my honest approach to confronting common leadership struggles (e.g., identifying "weeds" or nurturing team growth), while gaining hope for transformation.

You'll enjoy a blend of storytelling, research, and actionable steps that provide immediate practical takeaways. Each principle follows a clear, actionable template. We'll start with a brief explanation of the principle before diving into ***Implementing the Principle,*** a series of actionable steps you can take today. Then, you'll read about real-world leaders who have successfully applied this principle. And finally, ***you*** get the last word after every principle. You'll find four questions at the end of each principle to help you reflect on what you just read and discuss it with your team, friends, and family. I designed this actionable template specifically for you, a professional who values time and efficiency. That means *Lead Last* isn't just a book of fluff that collects dust on your shelf after one quick read; it's a concise guide to implement, teach, and live.

Overall, you will learn that leadership isn't about being the loudest voice in the room. It's about being the quiet force that lifts others and drives meaningful change. Imagine if a self-help book, a leadership conference, and a pep rally had a baby. That's what you are about to experience by reading this book! Are you ready to take that step?

Let's dive in!

PART 1
WHO ARE YOU?

This part might make some of you cringe, but stay with me. Many of us—including me—prefer to ignore the introspective side of leadership. It's easier to focus on *looking* the part, like King Leonidas, and projecting power. Frankly, that approach can work sometimes! Take high school basketball, for example. I was known to get pretty hype in my glory days, jumping, screaming, and dancing to pump up my teammates. It worked for those inspirational moments, but let me tell you: We didn't win games because of "Hype Man Lu" alone. Our success came from our coach's strategic leadership.

Effective leaders understand the difference between fleeting *moments* of inspiration and an *ongoing* lifestyle of influence. It's time to look introspectively so you can lead effectively.

The Danger of Insecure Leadership

Self-reflection isn't just helpful; it's essential for growing our *emotional intelligence* (i.e., mastery of our emotions and understanding others' emotions). Leaders with low emotional intelligence often become insecure, and insecure leadership is the root of many leadership failures.

We've all encountered insecure leaders before. They micromanage, can't take criticism, avoid dissent, hoard authority, demand credit for every success, and make what psychologists refer to as "defensive decisions." They may even come across as arrogant to hide deeper fears. Sound familiar?

Here's the tough part: These traits are easy to spot in others but difficult to see in ourselves. It took me *years* to recognize my insecurities, but once I did, I realized they stemmed from a deeper issue. I had to address the *root* of the problem.

The Mask of Insecurity: A Personal Example

I remember watching an old video of myself and cringing—not at the footage, but at the memory of my feelings in the clip. The video was from my sister's wedding. Everyone in the limo was smiling, laughing, and celebrating. When the camera panned to me, I had a camera in front of my face—hiding. You might think it was a joke at first glance, but I remember exactly how I felt at that moment: insignificant.

I was teased for my weight, the gap between my teeth, and even my name. Although my parents and family encouraged me, the negativity rang louder in my mind. I started to *identify* as the "flawed" version of myself, and I hid. Insecurity manifested in destructive ways, including rule-breaking, angry outbursts, and misbehavior at school. Those moments gave me a temporary sense of belonging because, for once, I wasn't being judged. But the relief never lasted.

As adults, we may find our insecurity shows up differently, but the patterns are familiar. Leaders who feel insecure may attempt to befriend everyone to be "liked," hoard information to stay in control, or become overly defensive to criticism and borderline paranoid if they feel someone is challenging their authority or gunning for their position. They blame others for failures they should own. Are you strong enough to admit if this sounds like you?

Many of us are so insecure and unsure of who we are that we are willing to do almost anything to divert attention from our flaws. This inevitably causes a rift between us and the people we lead because they can see their insecure (and sometimes perceptively incompetent) leader through the ruse. Insecure leaders' actions are often inconsistent, erratic, and unaligned with the position they hold and the person they were born to be. These behaviors create a toxic cycle, damaging relationships, undermining trust, and causing workplace instability.

At its core, insecurity is a shaky foundation. It leaves leaders feeling malleable, shaped by external forces, or brittle, breaking under pressure.

By contrast, stability brings strength. A stable leader is firm, resilient, and calm under pressure. They are tethered to their values, even in the face of challenges. Looking back, I can see how insecurity made me a reactive and inconsistent leader who chased approval instead of standing by my principles in my early leadership days.

I have great news, though: Growth is possible! However, to move forward, you must first answer one critical question:

Who Are You?

Why Identity Matters

You lead with confidence instead of fear when you know who you are. You become consistent, intentional, steady, and obsessed with pursuing a higher purpose—a leader people want to follow.

Chasing success leads to disappointment.
Chasing purpose leads to fulfillment.

By growing through insecurity, you're not just becoming a better leader—you're becoming the person you were meant to be. You're learning to live a fulfilling life and inspiring people along the way!

How to Overcome Insecurity and Find Your Identity

Finding your identity is about discovering and embracing your values, strengths, and purpose. Here's how to get started:

1. Self-Reflection: Look Inward

- **Purpose:** Live on purpose (i.e., develop habits that support peak physical, mental, emotional, and spiritual health) and for a purpose—your unique reason for being on this earth. Clearly define and declare your purpose by answering these three questions. The intersection of your answers reveals your inspiration and, ultimately, your purpose:

    - What activities, thoughts, or passions energize me?
    - What are my greatest strengths?
    - What value do I bring to those around me? (*Hint: We all bring value to those around us.*)

- **Values:** Adopt guiding principles like honesty, compassion, and perseverance. More than rules, these are the foundation for consistent decision-making.
- **Strengths and weaknesses:** Write them down. Start with the feedback you've received or challenges you've overcome. Be brutally honest but not overly critical of yourself.
- **Defining moments:** Reflect on life events that shaped your values and character. These moments reveal who you are at your core.

2. Feedback from Others: Look Outward

- **Friends and family:** Ask your inner circle what they see as your strengths. Accept both encouragement and *constructive* criticism.
- **Professional feedback:** Seek input from counselors, mentors, colleagues, and direct reports. They can provide insight into blind spots you and your inner circle may not notice (or refuse to acknowledge).
- **Online resources:** Tools like Myers-Briggs or CliftonStrengths can reveal hidden aspects of your personality.

Tip: Feedback is a tool, *not* a verdict. Use it to understand how others perceive you—not to define who you are.

3. Journaling: Track Your Growth

- **Daily reflections:** Write about situations that made you feel insecure and how you responded. Look for patterns over time and address the root of the problem.

4. Identify Your Passions

- **What excites you?** Think about activities or topics that energize you. Your passions often align with your identity and purpose. The key here is to identify true hobbies, **not** the things you do to mask your insecurities.

Now that we've set the foundation of self-awareness, you're equipped to learn and apply the practical leadership strategies in the following chapters. However, remember that effective leadership stems from continual growth. Don't attempt to *lead* through your insecurities; instead, *grow* through them to lead with a lasting impact.

PRINCIPLE #1

LET YOUR GUARD DOWN

Be a leader, not a stick in the mud.

It's okay to *reveal* your personal side. The keyword is *reveal*. That means you intentionally share personal anecdotes and information about yourself that can help bring the team together. Being kind, courteous, approachable, and friendly doesn't mean you have to befriend everyone and become a people pleaser. Just let your team see your human side.

Implementing Principle #1:

1. **Share funny and/or embarrassing stories.** This is a great way to be vulnerable with your team and open yourself up to a little humor. I enjoy playful banter and have been known to tease or lightheartedly "troll" my team members to keep things light. This fosters a more familial environment, where team members develop

genuine relationships and feel a deeper sense of commitment to one another.

2. **Discuss hobbies and interests.** Steer clear of the most common divisive topics, such as religion, health issues, and politics. Instead, stick to commonalities like sports, home décor, projects, weekend getaways, family activities, TV series, books, movies, etc. Find common ground and share your interests.
3. **Don't discuss it at the park if it happens in the dark.** Okay, that was my corny way of saying something that rhymes, so the point sticks in your mind. (That one was unintentional.) A good rule of thumb is to avoid conversations that can bring discredit to your family and close friends or reveal information that is sexual in nature or would be considered a private matter by a rational adult.
4. **Familial vs. familiar.** Don't get it twisted: Organizational structures exist for a reason. Developing a familial bond requires team members to get to know and care for one another, just as they would in a close-knit team. However, that requires maturity and mutual respect for each person, the position they hold, and the authority associated with that position. Being too familiar means we've overstepped professional bounds and begun disrespecting or disregarding the structure. This leads to toxicity in the workplace and disruptive behavior that detracts from the cohesiveness needed to accomplish shared goals.

Ironically, the latter key insight is why I would have given you the opposite advice on this principle several years ago. I wanted to project a stoic demeanor and a serious appearance. I wanted to emphasize the distinction between personal and professional relationships while demonstrating to everyone that I took my job seriously as a young leader. Over time, I realized that being my jovial self didn't detract from my ability to set and enforce high standards. My Marines know that I mean business, and we will accomplish the mission. However, we will do so as a close-knit team that can rely on one another through both thriving and challenging times. They know that there's no personal or professional problem that we cannot solve together and that I use this principle to build a cohesive team. Most importantly, we establish clear boundaries and expectations to maintain mutual respect and trust.

Tip: Be careful with your playful banter. One time, I started my regular playful banter with one of my team members, only to receive a negative response. Unbeknownst to me, his wife filed for divorce the night before, and my banter was unintentionally picking at an open emotional wound—though unrelated. I was fortunate that he respected me enough to address this head-on, given our previous connection; otherwise, I could have easily lost his buy-in due to my insensitivity. **That's why connection and mutual respect come before playful banter.**

Principle #1 in Action

A great real-life example of letting your guard down as a leader comes from Howard Schultz, the former CEO of Starbucks.

Schultz returned as CEO of Starbucks in 2008. That was during a period of declining sales and company morale. Consequently, he faced the *monumental* task of turning the company around. Some would expect a data-driven approach to turning the company around. Instead, Schultz decided to let his guard down by sharing personal stories about his upbringing and how his experiences shaped his leadership philosophy, rather than focusing solely on strategies and data. By doing so, Schultz created a more familial environment in which team members developed genuine relationships and felt a deeper commitment to one another.

In one particularly vulnerable moment, Schultz discussed his family and interests by sharing the story of his father, who worked as a truck driver without benefits. Schultz spoke about how his father's lack of healthcare and job security motivated him to ensure Starbucks employees were cared for, which led to Starbucks being one of the first companies to offer comprehensive healthcare and stock options to part-time workers (Schultz 1997).

This act of vulnerability resonated deeply with Starbucks employees and executives, reinforcing their belief in Schultz's commitment to their well-being. Schultz emphasized his commitment to his employees' well-being by visiting stores, talking with baristas, and listening to their concerns—making them feel heard and valued. By letting his guard down, he created a personal connection with employees that helped foster trust and loyalty. This was critical in rebuilding the company's culture and success. This is the same company that Schultz transparently told, "We are seven months away from insolvency."

Schultz undoubtedly made difficult decisions during this period, such as closing underperforming stores and restructuring management. He established clear boundaries, standards, and expectations to maintain mutual respect and trust with his team; however, his ability to balance these actions with transparent communication and a commitment to employee well-being highlights the power of authentic leadership in fostering trust and loyalty amidst organizational challenges. Schultz developed personal connections to build a cohesive team that felt valued and inspired.

The Last Word on Principle #1

- When was the last time you allowed vulnerability to strengthen trust with your team?
- What barriers prevent you from being more transparent with others?
- How might your leadership change if your team saw more of your authentic self?
- Who on your team needs to see that you trust them enough to be open with them?

PRINCIPLE #2

SHARE THE MOMENTS

Let your presence be a present to those around you.

Team cohesiveness allows you to be physically and emotionally engaged with your team members. Even so, many of us have led from opposite ends of the spectrum, depending on what was happening in our lives at the time. On one hand, we may be physically present, but our minds are elsewhere. We appear isolated and disconnected from our team and the world around us. In this case, we are living *at* the moment.

On the other hand, we follow the wind wherever it leads. We become so engrossed in our team members and current projects that we lose sight of the long-term vision and mission. Because of this, our relationships, interactions, and engagements are sporadic and inconsistent, and our decisions are often erratic, careless, and dangerous. Many may call us "scatterbrained." In this case, we are living *around* the moment.

I recommend you find a balance between these two extremes and live *in* the moment!

Implementing Principle #2:

1. **Seek closure from previous conversations, projects, and anything that preoccupies your mind.** Develop a daily *closure ritual* that completes a particular task or conversation. This is an intentionally scheduled time that concludes with you declaring the end of the activity, allowing you to become more engaged with those around you. I like to associate this step with a physical action.
2. **Structure your day . . . and your desk.** Zig Ziglar is widely attributed with this quote, "If you aim at nothing, you will hit it every time." Set daily goals and establish a "daily battle rhythm." The latter is a military term that describes the deliberate, repeatable events we do every day to achieve a specific goal. I recommend implementing CCTV: Checklists, Clocks, Timers, and Voices.

    a. **Checklists:** Many scientists recommend checklists because, according to them, our brain releases dopamine every time we check that tiny box. That dopamine creates positive feelings, which, in turn, give us the adrenaline we need to complete the next task. This keeps us focused, on time, and on target.
    b. **Clocks:** Allocate blocks of time to do certain tasks. At first, it may be tough to guess the time a task will take accurately, but you'll be able to create a better schedule as you continue to practice.

c. **Timers:** Having a scheduled time block is important, and sometimes seeing that time dwindle is the psychological *push* we need to complete various tasks. Additionally, the act of counting down creates an urgency that gives importance and relevance to each task. Some argue that urgency draws on our adrenaline supply while increasing anxiety. Contrarily, I submit that the adrenaline rush gives us the momentum and focus to complete a list of tasks on time. Using timers combines physical and psychological activities to produce a favorable reaction.

d. **Voices:** Listen to your voice and your accountability partner's voice. (Implied task: Assign yourself an accountability partner.) Sometimes, our thoughts tend to drown out our conscience. That's why we all need a colleague (or group of colleagues) to help hold us accountable. Listen to their feedback. As we learned earlier, it will expose blind spots.

3. **Don't be afraid to get your hands dirty.** I've worked various jobs, from chicken farms to waiting tables, to landscaping, so I know a thing or two about getting dirty. I've spent days *longing* to be covered in mud with my Marines to share their misery. Why? Getting your hands dirty means rolling up your sleeves, staying engaged, and demonstrating to your team that no task is beneath you. Make time to work alongside your team members. They need these inspirational moments to know that you're fully committed to accomplishing the mission. With that said, don't become so consumed

with today's problems that you lose sight of tomorrow. Living in the moment and "getting dirty" is an opportunity to inspire your team in your current situation, not an excuse to make careless decisions.

4. **Be the ~~man in the arena~~ leader in the conference room.** Theodore Roosevelt once said, "It is not the critic who counts; not the man who points out how the strong man stumbles, or where the doer of deeds could have done them better. The credit belongs to **the man who is actually in the arena**, whose face is marred by dust and sweat and blood; who strives valiantly. . ." (emphasis mine). Leaders can learn from this: You do not have to be the smartest, but as the leader, you must assemble the right people and **be in the room** to solicit the best solution. Though you may not originate every idea, your role in defining the problem, soliciting resources and expertise, setting boundaries, refining guidance, keeping your team focused on the solution, and maintaining momentum is critical. That's why you must remain committed and engaged throughout the problem-solving process. Your team (*and organization*) needs you in the room.

Principle #2 in Action

I experienced an amazing example of this when I was an intern turned computer programmer/analyst at Tyson Foods. Donnie Smith—the CEO at the time—would bring everyone together and say, "I don't have all the answers, but the answer is in the room." This simple statement demonstrated his commitment to remaining in the moment, being fully present with his team, and being **the leader in the conference room.**

There are several notable advantages to Donnie's strategy. For starters, he publicly acknowledged that, though he was the leader, he did not have all the answers. He also showed that he was willing to give everyone a voice—I, as the new, lowly intern, witnessed him say this multiple times. He accentuated this point by memorizing our names and the last project we were working on and mentioning it when he saw us in passing. Lastly, he demonstrated that he was fully committed to providing resources and helping to solve problems. He wasn't a stick in the mud, but was in the mud with us—getting his hands dirty when he needed to for the betterment of the company.

That's not all I admire about Donnie. Tyson acquired Hillshire Brands in 2014. As you can imagine, merging two major corporations like these takes time, patience, and diligence in every department, from marketing to IT to human resources. An acquisition of this magnitude requires all hands on deck, and all eyes are on the CEO as he continues to advance the company despite the inherent internal friction that comes with a merger. While I haven't seen his daily schedule from that time period, Donnie's actions strongly suggested that he had closure rituals, clearing his mind so he could give his full attention to the challenges at Tyson. It was also clear that he recognized the need to remain engaged, connected, and organized, providing guidance and direction throughout the process. The impressive part is that **he didn't lose sight of his obligations at home.**

One of my favorite quotes from Donnie is, "The term *work-life balance* is a mystery to me. I don't know anyone who day-in and day-out strikes a perfect balance. For me it's like a bank account. Sometimes I draw down on the balance like in recent months with this Hillshire acquisition, but I know that I can't let it get too low. I have to start making some deposits to rebalance the account. Like last night when the whole family spent nearly three hours at Mama Z's eating fried chicken and spaghetti. It took us about thirty minutes to eat and we spent the rest of time catching up."

Since leading last is about putting others first, we have to understand what that means in practice. Our commitments drive our priorities, and these commitments are organized according to our schedule. Use your schedule wisely, and like Donnie exemplified, know when and where you are supposed to be to make the most impact. Be the man or woman in the room who is influencing progress with his or her presence.

The Last Word on Principle #2

- How often do you pause to celebrate small wins with your team?
- What daily routines or traditions could you create to foster connection?
- Who is one person on your team you could intentionally recognize today?
- What would your team culture look like if moments of joy became the norm?

PRINCIPLE #3

LEAD BY SHARING GOALS

Sharing and achieving goals creates a ripple effect and builds momentum.

If you can't tell, I love the idea of leaders getting their hands dirty with their team members. It opens up opportunities to communicate and share personal insights. It also presents excellent opportunities to share personal and professional goals. (I'll tell you how to set and achieve goals shortly.) Jim Collins and Jerry Porras said it best in *Built to Last: Successful Habits of Visionary Companies*: we should set Big Hairy Audacious Goals (BHAG) (Collins and Porras 1994). These are goals that are intimidating, compelling, and scary but required to encourage you and your followers to continue on an upward trajectory toward success. Being a lifelong leader requires you to set and achieve BHAGs while articulating a clear mission and compelling vision for your team.

Transparently setting and achieving goals is a great way to encourage others to refine and streamline processes at work while consistently refining themselves in their personal life. As the structure of this book indicates, it all begins with knowing and mastering these concepts in our personal lives before we can apply them in the workplace.

Implementing Principle #3:

1. **Learn how to set and achieve goals. Codevelop professional goals with your team members.** It's time for another 1990s-esque corny acronym! Are you ready? Achieving goals is DOPE.

Figure 1. *D.O.P.E. Framework.*

a. **Dream:** You have to see yourself accomplishing whatever goal you set! Example: I see myself with a body ready to compete for the lead role in *Creed IV.*
b. **Offload:** Don't worry about structure or a template during this phase. Simply draw or write out your dream.
c. **Plan:** Begin with highlighting four legs or critical aspects of each dream. For example, if my dream is to build a body ready to compete for the lead role in *Creed IV*, the four legs I would identify are diet,

cardiovascular workouts, strength training, and rest. Then I would go through the first three phases (Dream, Offload, and Plan) for all four of those legs. We lay the groundwork for success by answering the following for each leg:

- **Define success and purpose.**
  - ✓ What does success look like?
  - ✓ Why does this goal matter?
  - ✓ How does it align with your purpose?

- **Assess your readiness.**
  - ✓ Are you physically, mentally, spiritually, and resourcefully prepared?

- **Identify key players.**
  - ✓ Who is involved?
  - ✓ Who needs to be involved?

- **Map out the process.**
  - ✓ What steps are required?
  - ✓ What's the timeline?

d. Execute. Measure and celebrate your progress, no matter how small it may seem. Keep pressing and pursuing your goals!

2. **Share your goals with your team.** You probably thought the *Creed IV* reference was a joke, but I did that! I even adopted a catchphrase and hashtag to share with my wife and team, "Michael B. Can't Beat

> Me" (#MBCBM). The more I talked about and pursued this goal, the more my team held me accountable. Interestingly, my team also began to share their personal fitness goals, which in turn led to other personal goals, which ultimately evolved into professional goals. We motivated each other to achieve our individual goals, and we leveraged that momentum to boost productivity at work. Win-win!

Principle #3 in Action

Looking back, it's amazing to see how we can feed off of each other's successes. I'd be lying if I pretended that I strategically shared my goals to inspire my team and spark a chain of positive events. It just sort of happened that way. Nevertheless, we can learn a lot from my team's response to my journey. Most of my Marines connected with the challenge associated with the audacious goal I set. It worked out well that they, too, could see my purpose and measure my progress. As I alluded to before, chasing purpose leads to fulfillment, which is why my progress energized them to set and pursue their own goals.

The psychological benefit and adrenaline you get from achieving personal goals naturally enhance your ability to complete tasks in the workplace. The endorphins released in your brain when you successfully achieve a goal make it addicting, which makes it a way of life. In essence, it made my job a lot easier, because I had people who were eager to meet objectives, exceed standards, and win the day. All I had to do was codevelop goals, provide guidance, and watch them work! *That's* the power that mastering goals has.

The Last Word on Principle #3

- Do your team members know what motivates you outside of work?
- How could sharing your goals help you model accountability?
- Which team members' goals could you ask about this week?
- What systems can you create to make goal-sharing a natural part of your culture?

PRINCIPLE #4

BE YOURSELF BUT ADAPT YOUR MANAGEMENT STYLE TO THE TEAM YOU HAVE

There's no "one-size-fits-all" management style.

Learning about your team members' personal and professional goals will give you a greater appreciation for the diverse perspectives and skills they bring to the table. Thriving organizations know the importance of recruiting and appointing a diverse group of leaders. Our various experiences and backgrounds give us a unique perspective with which we form our opinions and management styles. It's easy to settle into a comfortable style, especially when we achieve success over time. Therein lies my warning: The "one-size-fits-all" approach to management will frustrate your star performers and stagnate your average performers. That's why we should get to know our teams, understand what motivates them daily, and adjust accordingly.

Implementing Principle #4:

1. **Be flexible, not malleable.** To adapt and thrive in your environment, avoid becoming reshaped or transformed into a person that you're not, as people will see through your facade, and you will lose credibility. I learned this lesson during my first stint as an operations officer (OpsO). In my mind, a good OpsO was firm and straightforward, and when folks weren't doing what they were supposed to, he would chew them out! I operated under that pretense and was often rewarded with "positive" results.

   The problem was people were more inclined to do what I said to avoid being nagged, not because they were committed to the mission. That's like playing not to lose instead of playing to win. You want *buy-in* from the people you lead so they will be motivated to operate independently to accomplish the mission, instead of responding to fear or an unwillingness to be annoyed by their leader.

2. **Let your past experiences *inform* but not *dictate* your future.** Don't become a "back in my day" leader. Somehow, *every* generation anecdotally grew up at a time when things were better. Yet, the quantifiable data doesn't support that assertion. The various experiences we've had in life enhance our ability to quickly orient a problem to develop a solution, but they don't dictate the solution itself.

Don't automatically apply solutions from your past without examining the current problem *in context*. Instead, use those experiences to feed the brainstorming session as you codevelop solutions with your team.

3. **Let people tell you how to lead them best.** I learned this lesson from my dad. He was specifically referring to parenting, but the message is sage. There are many leadership books (including this one) that provide general advice to point you in the right direction, but your success lies in your ability to understand yourself, your environment, and the people you lead to apply the advice *in context*. The people you lead will give you feedback through verbal and nonverbal cues. Your job is to be humble enough to receive feedback and flexible enough to adjust and apply what you've learned.

Principle #4 in Action

Satya Nadella, CEO and chairman of Microsoft, is an exemplary leader who has adapted his management style while remaining true to his identity. Microsoft was known for its aggressive, highly competitive internal culture when Nadella became CEO in 2014. Many say that the company previously operated with a win-at-all-costs mentality, which often stifled collaboration and innovation. Recognizing this, Nadella shifted Microsoft's culture to focus on empathy, collaboration, and a growth mindset.

Nadella emphasized the importance of listening, understanding others' perspectives, and fostering a culture where employees feel valued and supported. There's a lot to love about his story, but my favorite part as a family man and founder of Parent-Child-Connect.com is how Nadella's approach to leadership is deeply rooted in personal experiences and family connections. He expressed the following in a passionate LinkedIn post about his family: "Anu is an amazing woman, mother and partner. Her empathy for others runs deep, and from her, I have learned that when I infuse empathy into my everyday actions it is powerful, whether they be in my role as a father or as a CEO."

He continued, "Becoming a father of a son with special needs was the turning point in my life that has shaped who I am today. It has helped me better understand the journey of people with disabilities. It has shaped my personal passion for and philosophy of connecting new ideas to empathy for others. And it is why I am deeply committed to pushing the bounds on what love and compassion combined with human ingenuity and passion to have impact can accomplish with my colleagues at Microsoft." (Nadella 2017).

From this, we can conclude that Nadella is comfortable with who he is and confident in his ability to lead Microsoft effectively and empathetically. Nadella cultivated a thriving environment to give his followers the resources they needed to grow without losing his identity. Here's a key point: Nadella "grew up" in Microsoft—he joined the company in 1992. However, his tenure as CEO and chairman reflects an individual who perpetually flexed his management style while refusing to be reshaped by the win-at-all-costs culture. Instead, he emphasized the importance of understanding others' challenges and needs.

Nadella's ability to adapt while staying true to himself revitalized Microsoft:

- The company's market value soared from around $300 billion in 2014 to over $2 trillion in 2023 (Yahoo! Finance n.d.).
- Microsoft became a leader in cloud computing, artificial intelligence, and collaborative tools like Microsoft Teams.
- The company's employee satisfaction and culture rankings significantly improved.

Nadella's story demonstrates that leaders can evolve their management styles to fit the needs of their organizations without compromising their core values and identity. His example highlights how authenticity and adaptability can drive personal and organizational success.

The Last Word on Principle #4

- In what ways do you naturally lead?
- Which parts of your style energize your team, and which parts might hold them back?
- How can you adjust without compromising your authenticity?
- Where do you see opportunities to flex your style for greater impact?

PRINCIPLE #5

BE STUDIOUS

A studious leader is a sturdy leader.

Great organizations are built and maintained by strong leaders like Nadella. These leaders' compelling vision inspires organizational members to achieve greatness, and their strategies are rooted in sound doctrine. All of this is made possible by being proficient in your vocation and industry. Plain speak: It's hard to lead someone in an environment you do not understand. You don't have to be the subject matter expert in every topic, but you should have a general understanding of each team member's role, what they provide to your organization, and how their contributions fit in the big picture. You may not be able to tell them the technical *how*, but you have to be able to tell them the *who*, *what*, *when*, *where*, and *why*.

Implementing Principle #5:

1. **Study what your peers and predecessors are doing and have done.** Former US secretary of defense and Marine Corps legend General James "Mad Dog" Mattis consistently highlighted the need for leaders to read and study to be effective. He and his coauthor, Bing West, assert in *Call Sign Chaos: Learning to Lead*, "If you haven't read hundreds of books, learning from others who went before you, you are functionally illiterate—you can't coach and you can't lead" (Mattis and West 2019). Studying others isn't extraneous or just another item on your "I'll get to that eventually" list. It's a requirement to be an effective leader.

2. **Be proficient in your profession.** Being competent and skilled in your profession allows you to perform your job effectively, efficiently, and confidently. More importantly, your awareness of current issues, successes, discoveries, and innovations in your specific industry gives your team members confidence in your abilities. Being proficient doesn't require you to have all the answers to every question, but you should at least understand well-known concepts and the basics of each team member's role. Proficiency increases efficiency and productivity.

3. **Study to diversify your knowledge and experience.** Intentionally submerging yourself into diverse cultures and industries gives you a wider range of perspectives

and approaches to solving problems. Take a look at your library. Do you notice a common trend or topic in your books? What about your recommended articles or documentaries? I get it, there are only twenty-four hours in a day, so finding time to study your profession *and* other professions is tough—especially if you lead in a highly technical industry. The solution: Add podcasts and audiobooks to your schedule. Start by finding podcasts and audiobooks that align with your personal and professional goals. Then, expand that to things you observe on a daily basis. Augmenting your studying with twenty to thirty minutes of listening to various topics while commuting, doing the dishes, or doing other activities will work wonders in diversifying your knowledge and experience.

Principle #5 in Action

Let's talk a little more about the legendary General Mattis. As I alluded to before, he is renowned for his deep knowledge of military history and for using historical battles to inform his strategies. For example, during the Iraq War, he often referenced the Battle of Thermopylae and the leadership of King Leonidas to inspire his troops and highlight the importance of discipline, unity, and resilience in the face of adversity.

Additionally, General Mattis studied the counterinsurgency tactics of T.E. Lawrence (Lawrence of Arabia) to guide his approach during operations in Afghanistan and Iraq. General Mattis tailored his strategies to prioritize relationship building with tribal leaders and minimize unnecessary collateral damage by studying Lawrence's emphasis on understanding and working with local cultures. *Winning hearts and minds* is a critical counterinsurgency strategy that aims to undermine support for insurgent groups by improving the attitudes of civilians toward the government. Studying the art of war and mastering the science of battle alone would not have achieved the strategic objectives we sought as a nation. As such, General Mattis had to indulge himself in various cultures and study relationship-building techniques to lead effectively. This was not an easy feat.

General Mattis famously carries a personal library of over six thousand books, which he drew upon to adapt historical lessons to modern warfare. As he often said, "It's not enough to study the wars that were fought; you have to study how they were fought." No, I'm not saying you have to amass a huge collection of books in your library to be an effective leader. I'm emphasizing that you have to amass a diversified knowledge base to maintain your edge and lead your team through complex problems.

The Last Word on Principle #5

- What topic, book, or skill do you need to study next to serve your team better?
- How do you model lifelong learning for those you lead?
- Where are you relying on outdated knowledge, and how can you refresh it?
- Who could you invite into your study routine to multiply growth?

PRINCIPLE #6

BE STABLE AND LEVEL-HEADED

Consistency creates clarity, and clarity builds trust.

Having a diversified knowledge base allows you to gain your team's trust; however, you must also *maintain* their trust. Have you ever tried to follow someone through unknown territory as they speed through traffic lights and make *wild* turns? I have! It eventually caused me to *lose* trust in their ability to lead me to my destination. That's exactly what it's like to follow a leader who is inconsistent in his thoughts and emotions or who explodes or cowers at any challenge. **Your ability to effectively manage your emotions is a clear indicator of your level of emotional intelligence.**

Your organization appointed you as a leader to be a sturdy foundation on which they can build their success, and your team members rely on your consistency and stability to guide them through calm *and* chaotic times. You cannot do this unless you are stable and level-headed.

Implementing Principle #6:

1. **Be intentional about when and how you communicate with your team.** Regardless of industry, we often work in fluid environments. The more fluid the environment, the more inclined we are to stay ahead of and communicate the changes. This isn't inherently wrong, since we want our team members to operate and make decisions using the latest information. But a problem usually arises when you don't have a set method or venue to relay this information. Instead, you rely on pop-up or pop-in meetings or technology.

   Stop the pop! Pop-up and pop-in meetings are the best way for your message to get lost in translation. Give your guidance and direction once, and force your team to align all non-emergent meetings and updates to the set schedule you provide. Develop measures of effectiveness that quantify whether the information and messages you send are being received across the organization. If not, find and eliminate the bottleneck or source of misinformation. Lastly, avoid overreliance on technology or the temptation to send bits of information via various means. Deliberately choose an information flow resource that works for your organization, and allow that to be the single source of information. Nobody likes working in an organization where information inconsistently flows from various sources.

2. **Take time to digest the problem before leading a deliberate discussion.** Don't be too quick to jump to conclusions or provide solutions before you fully understand the problem. Equally as important, ask detailed questions to prevent your team members from intentionally or unintentionally withholding information from you before you give guidance or make a decision. Course corrections are a regular part of any leader's responsibilities; however, reneging or completely changing directions because you failed to gather information will eventually cause your team members to lose trust in your ability to lead.

3. **Master your emotions.** The most effective leaders learn how to manage their emotions and prudently use their reactions to influence their team's behavior. I've had the displeasure of working with leaders who took their teams on a daily emotional roller-coaster ride. Roller coasters are built to be enjoyable, but it's not as enjoyable when you go up, down, and roundabout only to finish where you started in an environment where progress is mandatory.

   Feeling emotions in response to a given circumstance makes you human. However, effective leadership requires you to control your response to that emotion. Let's hinge on the most common emotion that impacts our leadership: anger.

Let's Talk About *You*!

Thinking through this scenario is crucial to developing an intentional response the next time you encounter a similar circumstance.

Have you ever lost your temper in the workplace? What triggered that emotion? How did you respond once it was over? How did your team members treat you when it was over? How would you respond to that same incident now that you're intentionally building your emotional intelligence to become stable and level-headed?

> **Tip:** I shared a simple but effective technique on my website (www.Parent-Child-Connect.com) that is relevant to this topic. Search for "Stimulus-Response Model" on my blog to read the full article.

Ask the 5 Whys. Simply put, this is how we get to the root of our perspective to understand why we responded the way we did. Reflect on your scenario and ask, "Why does this matter to me?" Here's a quick example:

- That guy cut me off!
  - ▸ Why does this matter to me?
- Because it was my turn!
  - ▸ Why does this matter to me?
- Because it isn't fair.
  - ▸ Why does this matter to me?

- Because he's taking advantage of me.
    - Why does this matter to me?

- Because I'm tired of being taken advantage of.
    - Why does this matter to me?

- Because I know my worth, and I don't like when people make me feel like I'm less than I'm worth.

This is how we identify the root, and from that root spawns many thoughts, emotions, and causes. Focus on that root and solicit help from your counselor to develop new neural pathways.

Principle #6 in Action

Whereas other animals instinctively react to the stimuli around them, our brains can critically think about the various stimuli (i.e., cues and triggers) and develop a response based on the environment we are in.

Dr. M. Scott Peck has a funny (but true) way to describe this phenomenon in his book, *Further Along the Road Less Traveled: The Unending Journey Toward Spiritual Growth*: "People sometimes ask me the most impossible—for example. 'Dr. Peck, what is human nature?' . . . and first answer I give is: 'Human nature is to go to the bathroom in your pants.' It really is. That is exactly the way each one of us started out, doing what came naturally and letting go whenever we felt like" (Peck 1993).

As proven by millions of potty-training toddlers each day, we can influence our stimulus-response cycle to grow our emotional intelligence. Frank Esser shared his thoughts related to this topic in an insightful article at the University of Zurich titled "Stimulus-Response Model." Therein, he states, "Similar to higher animals, human beings are endowed at birth with a uniform set of instincts that guide their ways of responding to the world around them" (Esser 2008). We can influence this stimulus-response effect through the application of free will or choice.

We do so by applying the techniques in the graphic below.

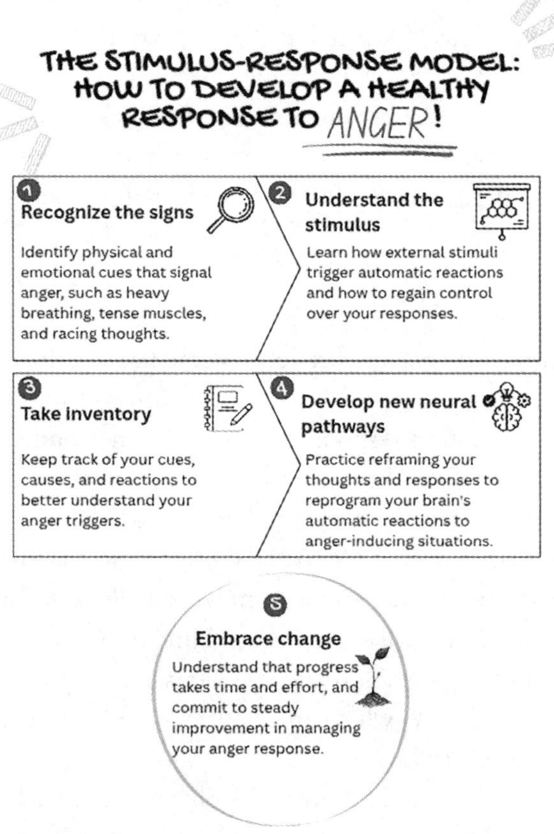

Figure 2. *The Stimulus-Response Model: How to Develop a Healthy Response to Anger.*

Real-world Example:

Let's talk about a real-world example of someone I witnessed walk through these steps. I'll change his name to protect his identity.

Meet "Brolaolu." He was leading a project kickoff meeting after weeks of pre-coordination and planning. Confident the meeting would be routine, he was caught off guard when a key player arrived angry, claiming Brolaolu's team was overstepping and piling on unreasonable expectations.

At first, Brolaolu stayed calm, but frustration quickly turned into anger. He lashed out with a sharp outburst, leaving the room silent. Though a colleague salvaged the meeting, Brolaolu knew he had lost control. Later, he pulled out his stimulus-response worksheet to reflect:

- **Signs:** heavy breathing, tense body, rising voice.
- **Triggers:** perceived personal attacks and disrespectful tone.
- **Pattern:** similar frustration surfaced the week before with someone else.
- **Reframe:** next time, slow down, assume positive intent, and seek clarity before reacting.
- **Commitment:** rehearse a calmer response, practice delaying judgment, and try to understand what they are trying to say and why they're saying it.

Some colleagues told him, "That needed to be said." But Brolaolu knew better. His role was to lead the meeting, not lose it. His self-reflection turned a misstep into growth, preparing him for the next challenge.

Your turn! I'm certain Brolaolu isn't the only one. Stable leaders don't earn trust because they're flawless; they do it by showing growth and control when it matters most. So, my challenge to you: How will *you* put principle #6 into action?

The Last Word on Principle #6

- How do you typically respond under pressure, and what does your team see?
- Which situations test your consistency most?
- What practices keep you grounded when emotions run high?
- How might greater stability change your team's trust in your leadership?

PRINCIPLE #7

ORGANIZATION IS KEY

"Plans are worthless, but planning is everything."

Dwight D. Eisenhower

Your ability to be stable and level-headed is largely dependent on how organized you are. Your schedule—or the lack thereof—communicates what or who you deem important. Have a system that allows you to be timely and precise. Don't allow the daily work schedule to disorient you due to your dishevelment. A leader must remain focused on the mission and not be distracted due to an inability to maintain a systematic approach to completing daily goals. Learning to be organized is key for effective leaders to influence people to accomplish the mission.

Implementing Principle #7:

1. **Budget your time like it's money . . . because it is.** "Remember that time is money. He that can earn ten shillings a day by his labour, and goes abroad, or sits

idle one half of that day, tho' he spends but sixpence during his diversion or idleness, ought not to reckon that the only expence *[sic]*; he has really spent or rather thrown away five shillings besides" (Franklin 1748).

Seldom do you find people who budget their time as they would their money. Ben Franklin's advice reminds us that there is a positive correlation between time and earnings, meaning that as the time spent working increases, so does the amount of money earned. That also means that we increase our potential earnings when we intentionally invest our time.

Accordingly, let's borrow Peter A. Pyhrr's *zero-based budgeting* technique from the financial industry to take charge of our daily affairs instead of wondering, "Where did the day go?" Here's a (nerdy) example of what that can look like:

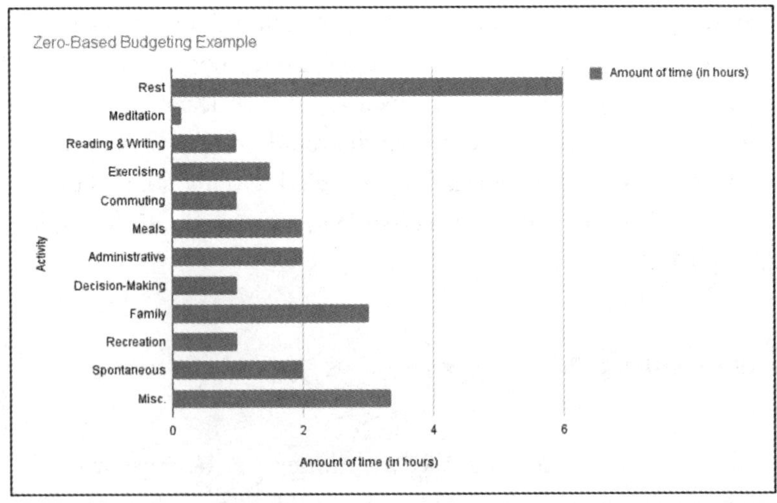

Figure 3. *Zero-Based Budgeting Example.*

2. **Use a calendar and a planner.** Now that you've budgeted every minute, write it down! I use a combination of Google Calendar and my work Outlook calendar to organize my personal and professional affairs. I'm careful to include reminders for things that require more time to ensure I'm in the right physical and mental state to complete the task. I use my calendar so often that I tell people, "My boss gives me guidance and intent, but my calendar tells me what to do every day." Using a calendar and/or planner increases efficiency and provides a daily executable plan for you to follow.
3. **Tidy up your workspace.** An organized workspace begets a more focused and productive leader. Though our perceptions don't always equal reality, many of us quickly judge a leader by what we see in his or her office—specifically if it's a junky office. Physically unorganized leaders tend to be scatterbrained. Effective leaders minimize distractions to allow easier access to necessary tools and documents, reduce mental clutter, and promote better focus. Ultimately, a tidier workspace creates a more streamlined workflow and improved productivity.

Tip: Respect people's time! For example, I've never been a fan of the "fifteen minutes early" methodology. This is where people show up fifteen minutes early to a meeting. This, in essence, means your team is sitting for fifteen unproductive minutes while they wait for you. Now, imagine a day where you have three to four meetings. That's forty-five to sixty unproductive minutes that you can't get back. I get it—encouraging people to show up "on time" will likely cause them to be late, and you fear you'd never start your meetings on time. Five minutes early is a happy medium. Regardless, the point remains: Stop wasting time!

Principle #7 in Action

A standout example of a leader whose success was driven by exceptional organizational skills is Dwight D. Eisenhower, the thirty-fourth president of the United States and supreme commander of the Allied Expeditionary Force during World War II.

Eisenhower's ability to plan and coordinate large-scale operations was critical to the success of the Allied forces. During World War II, he was responsible for overseeing the complex logistics and strategy behind Operation Overlord (D-Day), the largest amphibious invasion in history. Managing the invasion required meticulous coordination of diverse forces, including armies from different countries, thousands of ships and planes, and millions of people.

What set Eisenhower apart was his organizational discipline and ability to prioritize tasks. This philosophy reflected his belief that the process of organizing and preparing was more critical than the plan itself, and it allowed flexibility to adapt to unforeseen challenges. Here are some examples of how Eisenhower's organizational skills contributed to his ability to be an effective leader.

For starters, Eisenhower famously used what is now called the Eisenhower matrix. This is a time-management tool that prioritizes tasks based on urgency and importance. This system allowed him to focus on strategic decisions while delegating less critical tasks to others. The matrix reflects the philosophy of budgeting time like money:

1. **Important and Urgent:** Tasks he addressed personally.
2. **Important but Not Urgent:** Long-term planning he prioritized.
3. **Not Important but Urgent:** Tasks he delegated to others.
4. **Not Important and Not Urgent:** Activities he avoided altogether.

Eisenhower meticulously used calendars and planners to stay organized alongside his time-management tool. He scheduled every meeting, operation, and inspection to ensure nothing fell through the cracks in wartime and peacetime. This deliberate planning process reinforced his ability to lead complex operations effectively and keep his team on track.

Of course, this planning process wouldn't have been as effective if he hadn't kept an organized workspace. As a military leader, Eisenhower kept his desk famously tidy and his workspace always organized. **He believed that a cluttered environment led to a cluttered mind,** which could undermine decision-making. A clean workspace allowed him to approach problems with clarity, minimizing distractions and improving efficiency.

Eisenhower relied on structured chains of command and clear delegation protocols to handle routine matters in the military. He brought this organizational acumen to the White House. Eisenhower implemented a structured staff system to manage his administration effectively, delegating responsibilities to trusted aides while ensuring critical decisions remained under his purview. His ability to maintain order in both military and civilian leadership roles is a testament to the power of strong organizational skills.

The Last Word on Principle #7

- What systems currently help your team stay aligned and effective?
- Where does disorganization cost your team time or energy?
- How could you make your processes clearer for everyone?
- Which one area of your leadership needs greater structure right now?

Self-Discovery Is the Foundation

Eisenhower's example emphasizes the value of continuous learning, adapting, and preparing oneself to handle unforeseen challenges effectively. This is what mastering who you are and constantly seeking self-improvement is all about—preparing yourself to lead others through the unknown.

> Mastering our thoughts, emotions, and behaviors primes us for the next step: getting to know who you are leading.

PART 2

WHO ARE YOU LEADING?

We all come from different backgrounds and experiences, and together, these shape how we see and interact with the world. That's why Part 1 focused on introspection and self-awareness: Before we can understand others, we must become, as William Ernest Henley wrote, "the master of [our] fate" and the "captain of [our] soul."

But leadership doesn't stop there. Once you've laid a foundation of self-discovery and growth, the next question is, *Who are you leading?* The answer begins with the people right in front of you—your team, peers, even your family. To lead them effectively, you must build relationships founded on trust.

That's where the ***emotional bank account*** comes in. Every interaction is either a deposit or a withdrawal in the trust you share with others. By paying attention to those deposits and withdrawals, you'll discover not just *who* you are leading, but *how well* you are leading them. Let's dive a little deeper into that concept.

The Emotional Bank Account

I love reading! Though I don't have a favorite genre, I often gravitate toward books on leadership, biology, and relationships. Of these, the most useful to my daily life as a husband, father, Marine, and mentor are those focused on relationships. One recurring concept in many relationship books and classes is the metaphor of the *emotional bank account.*

I first encountered this idea through Dr. Stephen R. Covey, one of my favorite authors. In *The 7 Habits of Highly Effective Families*, he beautifully explains: "By proactively doing things that build trust in a relationship, one makes 'deposits.' Conversely, by reactively doing things that decrease trust, one makes 'withdrawals.' The current 'balance' in the emotional bank account will determine how well two people can communicate and problem-solve together" (Covey 1997).

This metaphor captures so much about how relationships thrive—or falter. **We're either depositing into or withdrawing from someone's emotional bank account in every interaction.** As leaders, our mission is to ensure those we lead have well-funded accounts. Why? Because healthy relationships create ripple effects. One positive relationship inspires another, leading to greater collaboration, loyalty, and success.

But how do we make those deposits? Let's examine seven key ways: love, compassion, peace, patience, knowledge, shared values, and redemption and restoration.

Making Deposits into the Emotional Bank Account

Category 1. Love: The Root of All Deposits

At its core, love is selfless sacrifice—giving your time, service, and energy to others. True love is patient, kind, and enduring, as described in 1 Corinthians 13:4–7. It's about empathy, understanding, and engagement. Love in the workplace is always a tricky (even taboo) concept, because we've intertwined it with romantic love. However, there's a mountain of research that supports the assertion that employees perform better when they feel loved. Here's some of the research:

- Google's Project Aristotle research determined that psychological safety—an environment where employees feel safe to express themselves without fear of embarrassment or retribution—is key to building an effective team. Acts of love, such as empathy, understanding, engagement, and inclusivity, contribute to this safety (The Google re:Work team n.d.).
- According to Businessolver's 2020 State of Workplace Empathy Executive Summary, 93 percent of employees say

that they are more productive when their leader selflessly recognizes their accomplishments (Businessolver 2020).

Leaders who demonstrate love build a foundation of trust and loyalty in their relationships.

> **Try this today!** Listen **without distractions**, offer support for a colleague working through a difficult task or situation, and search for ways to put others' needs ahead of your own.

Category 2. Compassion: Validation and Empathy

Compassion means validating and valuing others' thoughts, feelings, and experiences. It's not about fixing their problems, but showing empathy and understanding. Jane Dutton and her colleagues in the CompassionLab at the University of Michigan suggest that leaders who demonstrate compassion toward employees foster individual and collective resilience in challenging times (Lilius et al. 2013). For example, simply acknowledging a team member's disappointment in not achieving a personal goal might seem small, but it demonstrates care and connection, letting them know they have a supportive community to help them through difficulties.

> **Try this today!** Actively listen to others' concerns, validate their emotions, and show a genuine desire to help.

Category 3. Peace: Respect and Understanding

Unity, Turds: That is the key word in unit, without the y.

Major Benson Winifred Payne

Peace isn't the absence of conflict but the creation of mutual respect and understanding. We play an *active*—intentional—role in ensuring our teams unify for a common purpose or goal. Effective leaders prioritize unifying their teams because success is a byproduct of cohesiveness. Doing so fosters a productive, positive environment where everyone feels safe to contribute and thrive.

> **Try this today!** Listen **to understand**, eliminate judgment, and find common ground to create a culture of respect and dignity.

Category 4. Patience: The Quiet Strength

Patience requires action—it's choosing to accept delays or mistakes without frustration and trusting in the long-term growth of those you lead. Some of the most phenomenal leaders that I've had the pleasure of mentoring required a truckload of patience! Yet, I had to give them space to make mistakes, grow from their mistakes, and create momentum in their lives. Constantly hovering over a future star performer, or taking over instead of letting them figure it out will stunt their growth. *Everyone* is a work in progress, and patience creates space for others to learn and improve.

Try this today! Practice active listening, optimism, and grace when addressing challenges. Resist the urge to take over and complete the task yourself just because you can do it more quickly or efficiently. Celebrate progress, no matter how small.

Category 5. Knowledge: The Foundation of Growth

Knowledge is both experience and education. Leaders should create environments where others can grow through hands-on experiences and ongoing learning. For example, I've been known to create new challenges for my most talented Marines. I often assign challenging tasks that are loosely connected to their primary job. Doing so forces them to expand their knowledge, exercise the inventive portion of their brains, and develop into well-rounded professionals.

Try this today! Invest in teaching and training opportunities that build confidence and critical thinking in those you lead.

Category 6. Shared Values or Unifying Beliefs: The Glue of Relationships

Shared values are the principles that guide decisions and behavior. Coach Deion "Prime" Sanders does this extremely well! He adopts mantras like "I believe" for his players and fans to get behind. This unifying point encourages each team member to fulfill his or her role in accomplishing the overall mission while creating a bond that reminds team members that they are not alone. Leaders must identify, demonstrate, and enforce these values consistently. Here's an illustration you can use to align your team to shared values:

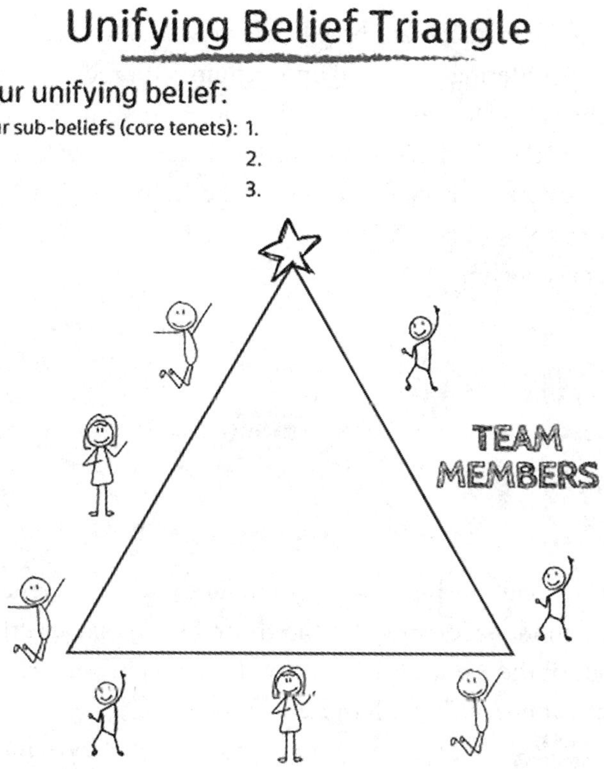

Unifying Belief Triangle

Our unifying belief:

Our sub-beliefs (core tenets): 1.
2.
3.

TEAM MEMBERS

Figure 4. *The Unifying Belief Triangle.*

> **Try this today!** Clearly articulate your values and work collaboratively to establish a shared value system that informs decisions and actions.

Category 7. Redemption & Restoration: Growth Through Grace

Mistakes are inevitable, but how leaders respond to them defines the relationship. Offering grace and opportunities for redemption teaches accountability and fosters deeper connections. Accountability is a must in the workplace, but don't be too quick to throw the book at someone. Learn the difference between mistakes and character flaws (we'll discuss this soon) and administer fair and judicious—not necessarily equal—consequences.

> **Try this today!** Turn mistakes into learning opportunities by helping others restore trust and confidence through accountability and corrective action.

Healthy relationships are the foundation of effective leadership, and these emotional deposits lay the groundwork for impactful leadership. Your ability to lead depends on how much trust, respect, and confidence you've built with those you serve.

Now, let's shift our focus from foundational relationship building to how leaders apply those principles in real-world settings. The following leadership principles build on the relational deposits outlined above to answer an essential question: **Who are you leading, and how do you help them thrive?**

PRINCIPLE #8

EVERYONE'S BACKGROUND IS IMPORTANT

Experiences shape solutions.

Get to know people by understanding where they're from, their values, their educational background, and their hobbies. This understanding should begin during the early stages (e.g., the interview process) and continue as you build your relationships. Research shows that teams that learn to respect and incorporate each team member's diverse background and perspective can solve problems faster and perform more efficiently. Effective leaders use this to their advantage to develop cohesive teams capable of quickly solving problems and efficiently accomplishing daily goals.

Implementing Principle #8:

1. **Ask your team members open-ended questions about their lives, upbringing, and experiences.** Asking open-ended questions encourages your team members to open up and share more about themselves. There

are three things you have to remember to make this work: Be genuine, be consistent, and be natural.

a. *But how?* Great question! After all, I wouldn't want you to find yourself in an awkward or unprofessional situation. There's a time and place for everything, so as a general rule of thumb, work during work hours. Use your regular one-on-one sessions, team-building events, or pre-coordinated lunches as a time to ask questions that give you better insight into who the person is without blurring the line between personal and professional. These questions are best suited for voluntary, casual conversations where the team member has the freedom to share as much (or as little) as they want. Here are a few questions to get you started:

   i. **Background and Upbringing:**

      1. What's one tradition from your family or childhood that you still carry with you today?
      2. What's one thing (or value) you learned from your hometown that shaped who you are today?
      3. What's a value you learned growing up that still guides your decisions?

   ii. **Experiences and Lessons Learned**

      1. What's the most meaningful lesson you've learned from a past experience (work or personal)?
      2. Tell me about a time you overcame a big challenge. What did you learn from it?

3. What's a lightbulb or pivotal moment in your life that made you proud of how far you've come?

iii. **Passions and Interests**

1. What do you enjoy doing outside of work that energizes you?
2. If you could learn a new skill or hobby right now, what would it be?
3. What's a goal you're working toward outside of work?
4. *Bonus* If you were a superhero, what would your superpower be? What is your superpower now?

iv. **Culture and Connection**

1. What's a holiday, tradition, or cultural practice that's important to you?
2. How do you like to celebrate milestones or successes?
3. What's one thing you wish people better understood about your background or perspective?
4. *Bonus* What kind of support makes you feel most valued?

2. **Observe.** Rachel Cruze said it best, "More is *caught* than *taught*." Pay attention to how each team member interacts in social and professional settings. What do you notice about their workspace, nonverbal cues, appearance, and personal style? You're not using this information to judge or form a biased opinion about

someone. You're using it to gain insight into what (or who) they value, their heritage and culture, and even their confidence and emotional state.

3. **Capitalize on each team member's strengths and supplement their weaknesses.** Codevelop a list of strengths and weaknesses for each team member after you've had an opportunity to observe them. Then actively search for daily opportunities to allow each team member to *flex* their strengths. Concurrently, capitalize on the dualities of your team members' strengths and weaknesses. In essence, you'll improve strengths through repetition and complement weaknesses through team collaboration.

Quick aside: There are two points I want to highlight

- **Merit-based recruiting is imperative.** The most qualified candidate should get the job, promotion, opportunity, etc. One thing to consider is that there's also such a thing as *convenient recruiting*, where candidates are selected simply because they are the most qualified *and* easily accessible person. Over time, this shortcut often produces homogenous teams. The same dynamic can happen once people are hired. Leaders who only listen to those closest to them by job title, appointment, or sheer outspokenness limit the value of the whole team. Effective leaders push past convenience, intentionally seeking out the best people and drawing out the best ideas from everyone.
- **We cannot overlook or undervalue the experience and background each team member brings to the table.** Our unique backgrounds shape how we solve problems and approach challenges. These qualities aren't always easy to measure, but ignoring them can come at a high cost.

Principle #8 in Action

I'm taking you back in time by using *Captain Planet* as an example to illustrate the idea of combining everyone's unique background to accomplish your organization's mission.

Scenario

Imagine a leadership team facing a major challenge: improving a company's sustainability practices. Each team member brings unique strengths but also has gaps in knowledge or skills. To solve the problem, they must collaborate and "combine their powers," much like the Planeteers in *Captain Planet.*

Strengths and Weaknesses

- Leader A is excellent at strategic planning but lacks environmental expertise.
- Leader B has deep knowledge of sustainability practices but struggles with communication and team alignment.
- Leader C excels in marketing and outreach but lacks data-driven decision-making skills.
- Leader D is great at operations and execution but lacks creative vision.

But with their powers combined, each leader contributes their unique abilities:

- Leader A sets the overarching strategy, ensuring the initiative aligns with the company's goals.
- Leader B provides detailed sustainability insights and recommends effective environmental solutions.
- Leader C creates a compelling public relations campaign to gain customer and stakeholder buy-in.
- Leader D ensures the plan is operationalized effectively, meeting deadlines and staying within budget.

Their combined skills create a comprehensive and impactful sustainability initiative that none could have achieved alone.

Create Captain Planet Moments!

Captain Planet emerges when the Planeteers combine their powers. He's able to overcome obstacles with abilities none of them have individually. Similarly, your team's synergy allows them to address every aspect of any given challenge. Whether you grew up watching *Captain Planet* or not, the idea is universal: When unique strengths combine, the result is far greater than any individual effort. Your effective leadership helps your team members overcome their weaknesses through collaboration.

The Last Word on Principle #8

- What one tradition, value, or experience from your upbringing still shapes how you work today?
- Who on your team brings a perspective you haven't tapped yet, and how can you invite that voice into a current project?
- When has a background difference caused a misunderstanding on your team, and what did you learn from that moment?
- What small, specific step will you take this week to learn one team member's story better?

PRINCIPLE #9

CANCEL COMPLAINING

A complaining culture is a toxic culture.

There's a disruptive action that destroys synergy: complaining. Problems deserve a solution based on facts, not whining based on emotions. Complaining sows seeds of discord and distrust, and it detracts from our ability to unify our team. Complaints—especially when heard out of context—can tear *any* team apart.

Implementing Principle #9:

1. **Know the difference between giving feedback and complaining.** I struggled with this concept as a new leader, because it seemed like a catch-22: I had to give each team member a voice to be an effective leader, but giving some team members a voice would inevitably lead to complaining, which I shouldn't allow. Time

and experience taught me that giving someone a voice doesn't equal allowing them to say whatever is on their mind. It means giving them *a means* to provide input. Each team member's input should provide a solution to a problem or an actionable idea to streamline processes. Contrarily, complaints glorify the problem and usually have a sarcastic undertone. Don't accept them.

a. Examples of complaints vs. feedback:

i. Redirect "This new system sucks and slows me down" to "This new system takes me three extra steps. Can I suggest a shortcut that would save time?"

ii. Redirect "Management never listens to us, so what's the point?" to "I'd like to propose a way we can share ideas with leadership more consistently."

iii. Redirect "We never do anything fun together." to "Can we plan one family activity each week where we all decide together?"

iv. Redirect "These training exercises are pointless" to "I don't see how this exercise connects to our mission. Could you help me understand, or could we revamp it to match real-world scenarios?

v. Redirect "We're always stuck with the worst shifts" to "Could we look at rotating shifts differently to balance the load across the team?"

This isn't just an argument of semantics; it's a shift in perspective that enables your team to develop actionable solutions. Over time, this shift helps prevent a toxic culture and creates a team trained to solve problems instead of dwelling on them.

2. **Venting is unhealthy and unhelpful.** Venting is a timeless process that doesn't work. Brad J. Bushman's research in "Does Venting Anger Feed or Extinguish the Flame? Catharsis, Rumination, Distraction, Anger, and Aggressive Responding" helps us understand that venting isn't a healthy release—it's a behavior that can perpetuate frustration and harm relationships within a team (Bushman 2001). It causes rumination on negativity, it doesn't address the problem, and the negativity is often burdensome to the listener. Instead, we should redirect our teams' focus toward healthier emotional management strategies, such as constructive feedback, active listening, and collaborative problem-solving. These approaches help preserve trust and harmony while addressing underlying issues.
3. **Publicly cancel complaining.** Effective leaders emphatically cancel complaining. Your team members need to understand that complaining is not allowed because it is not conducive to productivity. Pay attention to *how* you emphasize this point. Be firm but respectful. Say something like, "Thank you for your input, but what *actionable* steps are you recommending?" This encourages your team members to speak up when they have usable input without giving the impression that you are unwilling to listen to feedback.

Principle #9 in Action

I've seen what happens when complaints go unchecked, and it's not pretty. I always wanted to be perceived as the leader who is open to feedback, as I alluded to before. Accordingly, I rarely interrupted people when they ranted about policies, other leaders, the unit, the Marine Corps, and society in general. This was a healthy opportunity for them to vent their frustrations behind closed doors as they "complain up"—a concept that discourages leaders venting their frustrations in front of subordinates. I had great intentions and thought I was being the leader they needed.

In one particular case, I recognized that morale across the unit was dropping. I overheard more and more people venting frustrations, and productivity was decreasing. My initial reaction was to blame the environment we were in, because Marines are known for training and operating in austere environments. I was fully committed to that logic until I heard something familiar—it was the exact phrase one of my direct reports used during one of his venting sessions. I started hearing it over and over throughout my unit, spreading like an invasive weed. My inaction was causing morale and productivity to decrease.

It was obvious that I had work to do. I started by acknowledging the complaints and saying things like, "Let's do something about that." I eventually transitioned to saying, "We're part of the 'system' you're referring to. What are we going to do about it?" When that didn't work, I became more direct: "We (you and I) are the problem. What are we going to do about it?" He got the point—whining time was over. We began to improve morale by canceling complaining as a team slowly but surely. Correspondingly, productivity increased. We were able to identify the root cause of the problem and implement processes to improve our situation. That was only made possible by our joint effort to cancel complaining. This experience taught me that I didn't have to "shut him down" to cancel complaining. I needed to teach him to channel his voice into solutions.

The Last Word on Principle #9

- How do you tell the difference between complaint and constructive feedback in real time?
- Which recurring complaint on your team can be turned into an actionable project, and who will own it?
- What phrase will you use next time someone starts to complain to redirect them toward a solution?
- How will you publicly reinforce that complaining is canceled while still preserving space for honest input?

PRINCIPLE #10

IDENTIFY AND MEET EACH TEAM MEMBER'S NEEDS

Leading is recognizing that team members have the same mission but different needs.

Some of you are inspired to try a different approach after reading "Principle #9 in Action." Some of you are thinking, *Been there, tried that, and it didn't work*. Fair point. . . But what if the problem isn't that the person doesn't want to change or improve? What if the problem is that we don't fully understand what they need to do so? That's the real challenge of leadership: Each team member has different personalities, values, and experiences, and those differences shape what they require from you.

Effective leaders take the time to identify who needs what, communicate with clarity, and deliver the right support at the right time. Get this wrong, and frustration festers. Get it right, and you unlock performance, trust, and loyalty.

Implementing Principle #10:

1. **Grow your team members through collaboration.** Evolutionary psychology and research on human behavior support the claim that human nature inclines us to seek challenges and desire to be part of a team. For example, an article in *Trends in Cognitive Science* titled, "Born to Choose: The Origins and Value of the Need for Control" asserts that our belief that we are capable of producing desired results incentivizes our desire to be challenged (Leotti et al. 2010). Additionally, an article in *Psychological Bulletin* titled "The Need to Belong: Desire for Interpersonal Attachments as a Fundamental Human Motivation" highlights, "The desire for interpersonal attachments—the need to belong—is a fundamental human motivation" (Baumeister and Leary 1995). Collaborative problem-solving and social interaction are crucial for our survival, leading to an innate predisposition for teamwork. Effective leaders use this to their advantage, not by managing collaborative efforts in real time, but by seeking challenges and creating opportunities for team members to work and grow together.

2. **Don't excuse poor performance or behavior.** Whether by choice or by lack of skill, poor performance and behavior deteriorate collaborative efforts. In turn, you lose synergy and productivity. There's no wonder why so many senior leaders told me that their biggest mistake as a young leader was failing to fire their poor

performer sooner. We often excuse poor performance when the person appears to be favored by the rest of the team or if the person has more time in the organization than we do. Even worse, many of us fear confrontation or allow our personal biases to interfere with our ability to do what's best for the team. Effective leaders address this behavior directly. That means communicating clear expectations, providing support, and holding team members accountable when they fall short. Sometimes these conversations will spark real improvement; other times, despite your best efforts, they won't. When that happens, harder decisions may be required, and we'll address those in the next principle.

3. **Praise in public, poke in private.** I love recognizing my Marines for even the smallest reasons. One example is the Good Conduct Medal (aka "Good Cookie")—an award given to enlisted Marines who have served honorably and faithfully for three years while on active duty. Whether it's their first or fifth Good Cookie, I've been known to bring everyone together to recognize the award recipient. Some people push back by emphasizing that the Marine simply did his or her job and "didn't get caught" doing wrong. (The latter part of that sentence is usually said tongue-in-cheek.) My rebuttal is that we would have publicly reprimanded the Marine if they had gotten in trouble, so why not emphasize positive behavior, too? Public recognition goes a long way. Public praise reinforces positive behavior, boosts morale, and motivates others to perform well. Concurrently, private reprimands allow for a more constructive

conversation without the potential for embarrassment or defensiveness that can come with public criticism.

a. **When is it okay to reprimand in public?** There are a couple of notable exceptions to this rule.

  i. **When there's a cultural problem:** Attack the action, not the person or group of people. Have a private, constructive conversation with the wrongdoer(s). Publicly address the wrongdoing instead of the wrongdoer. Try not to even mention names in this circumstance.

  ii. **When the wrongful act brings public discredit to your team or organization:** Sometimes, you have to publicly disassociate your team or organization's culture and values from the wrongful acts of a team member. In this case, it is okay to mention a name—which will be perceived as public reprimand. Be concise and pure in your intentions. Say something like, "Mr. X's actions were of his own accord and not in keeping with Organization Y's culture and values of [your values]." By doing so, you are sharing a name for context, but the focus remains on reinforcing positive behavior and motivating others to perform well and in line with your organization's values.

Principle #10 in Action

Let's work through another scenario.

Scenario

A department manager, Sarah, is leading a project team tasked with launching a new product. The team consists of a few high-potential employees who are eager to contribute. There's one lovable team member, Mike, who consistently misses deadlines, undermines others' ideas, and shows no initiative to improve. He has been with the company for seventeen years, and his charisma makes him a fan favorite amongst other team members.

How can Sarah apply Principle #10 given this team dynamic?

1. **Grow team members through collaboration:** Sarah focuses on developing her high-potential team members by fostering collaboration. She encourages brainstorming sessions where everyone's ideas are valued, assigns challenging tasks to those ready for challenges, and provides mentorship to help team members grow. Example: Sarah notices that Lisa, a junior team member, has innovative ideas but lacks confidence. She partners Lisa with an experienced mentor and assigns her a leadership role on a smaller task to build her skills and confidence.

2. **Don't excuse poor performance:** Sarah addresses Mike's poor performance directly. She holds a one-on-one meeting to outline specific issues, provides

constructive feedback, and offers a performance improvement plan with clear metrics and a timeline. Example: She tells Mike, "Your missed deadlines have set us back by a week. To move forward, we need you to deliver X by Y date. If you don't meet this expectation, we'll need to reevaluate your role on this team." Mike isn't happy about this, but this constructive meeting is brief and concise. Sarah sticks to the facts, remains unemotional, and does not give in to Mike's charm or attempts to intimidate her using his longevity with the company.

3. **Praise in public, poke in private:** As the project progresses, Sarah praises the team members who excel and make meaningful contributions. She also enforces accountability when Mike fails to meet his improvement plan. Example: At a team meeting, Sarah says, "I want to acknowledge Lisa for her outstanding work on the market analysis. It's setting the tone for our campaign. However, we need everyone on this team to pull their weight. Missed deadlines and lack of collaboration can't continue."

Outcome

The team thrives as Sarah pours her energy into developing the high-potential employees. Despite multiple opportunities to improve after several formal constructive conversations, Mike continues to underperform. Sarah ultimately decides to terminate his employment. This decisive action eliminates the weed and allows the rest of the team to flourish, meeting and exceeding project goals.

This example demonstrates how effective leaders can balance nurturing talent while holding others accountable to protect the overall mission.

The Last Word on Principle #10

- Who on your team currently needs more clarity, confidence, resources, or stretch assignments, and which of those four will you prioritize for them?
- How will you document and communicate each person's primary need so that it's not forgotten after your one-on-one meeting?
- Of the support you've provided recently, which showed a measurable improvement and what made it work?
- If a person doesn't improve after targeted support, what is the next step you'll take (and when)?

PRINCIPLE #11

TRAINING DEFICIENCIES CAN BE REMEDIED; CHARACTER FLAWS CANNOT

Weed out what training and coaching can't fix.

How did Sarah know it was time to weed Mike out of her flourishing team? She recognized that he was absorbing precious team resources without providing value. Instead, Mike's actions were *straining* resources and *strangling* progress, and thus, each team member's individual growth. As with her other team members, Sarah provided mentorship, training, and a continuing education plan that addressed each deficiency. Some team members, like Lisa, took advantage of this program and grew. Mike did not.

There's an important contrast here: Lisa had training deficiencies; Mike had character flaws. Effective leaders must become skilled in recognizing the difference. Training deficiencies occur when a team member lacks a particular skill or set of skills required to fulfill a role. These are usually remedied by a systematic program that addresses the deficiency by teaching the required skills.

Conversely, some deficiencies are caused by "character flaws." *Oxford Languages* defines *character* as "the mental and moral qualities distinctive to an individual" (Oxford n.d.). These distinctive qualities influence each of our behaviors and daily decisions. Thereby, a *character flaw* is "a person's qualities, beliefs, and principles that influence the person to be unaligned with an organization's vision and values."

Like Sarah, effective leaders should meet deficiencies and flaws head-on and give the individual an opportunity to correct his or her deficiencies. However, refrain from sinking all of your time and efforts into trying to train someone who is unable or unwilling to accept your training—or worse, sinking them into trying to reconstitute someone whose beliefs and values are misaligned with your organization. That can cause you to lose focus on developing the rest of your team and achieving objectives. Sometimes, you just have to weed the individual out so you can focus on training and mentoring the rest of your team.

In this context, *weeds*—people who drain resources and degrade the team's ability to accomplish the mission—have an uncanny way of strangling progress and discouraging even the brightest and most talented people. *Uproot* them and focus your efforts on developing everyone else.

Implementing Principle #11:

1. **Customize your training and mentorship.** Our diverse backgrounds give us varying perspectives, and those varied perspectives cause us to learn differently. A tailored training and mentorship program should cater to each individual's specific career goals and learning style while addressing needs, strengths, and weaknesses. Here's a Nurturing Growth Cheat Sheet you can use to create customized training plans:

NURTURING GROWTH CHEAT SHEET

Skills Assessment and Individual Goals

Identify Strengths: Assess core competencies and talents.

Address Weaknesses: Determine areas for improvement to create a tailored plan.

Align Goals: Set individual goals that align with the mission and the team member's career aspirations.

Training Programs

Technical Skills Development: Provide specialized training relevant to the role.

Soft Skills Development: Include leadership, communication, and teamwork training.

Cross-Training Opportunities: Encourage learning in areas outside their primary responsibilities to foster adaptability.

Mentorship Plan

Identify Mentors: Pair team members with experienced professionals who can guide them.

Create a Structured Relationship: Establish regular check-ins and clear mentorship objectives.

Reverse Mentorship: Encourage younger employees to mentor more senior ones in areas like technology or emerging trends.

Continuing Education

Formal Education: Support further studies or certifications related to their field.

Conferences and Seminars: Fund attendance at industry events to expand knowledge and networking opportunities.

Online Learning Platforms: Offer access to tools like LinkedIn Learning, Coursera, or industry-specific training resources.

Experiential Learning

Stretch Assignments: Assign challenging tasks or projects that push team members outside their comfort zones.

Job Shadowing: Allow team members to shadow others in different roles to gain new perspectives.

Rotational Roles: Implement role rotation to build versatility and cross-functional knowledge.

Regular Feedback and Evaluation

Frequent Check-Ins: Schedule quarterly or monthly progress reviews to evaluate performance and update the plan.

Celebrate Successes: Acknowledge milestones and achievements to boost morale.

Adjust Plans: Refine goals and training strategies based on progress and team needs.

Leadership Development

Leadership Training: Offer programs focused on strategic thinking, decision-making, and team management.

Delegation of Authority: Gradually assign leadership responsibilities to prepare them for higher roles.

Focus on Work-Life Balance

Holistic Development: Incorporate wellness programs to ensure employees maintain a healthy work-life balance.

Example: Offer mindfulness workshops, time-management training, or flexible work arrangements.

Figure 5. *Nurturing Growth Cheat Sheet.*

2. **Don't outsource your key leadership opportunities.** Leaders at all levels are becoming increasingly comfortable with passing off leadership challenges to someone else. I'm an advocate for professional counseling and advice, but I've seen many leaders use this to replace a relationship with team members. Consequently, they are unable to find what motivates a team member who has the potential to excel. Overreliance on these resources can erode a critical part of being an effective leader: building genuine relationships. Don't delegate this core responsibility; instead, use leadership challenges as opportunities to go beyond surface-level interactions to learn more about your team members' motivations, struggles, and potential. Outside counseling should be a tool in the leader's toolkit, not a substitute for engagement.

3. **Weed out those who demonstrate character flaws—even when it hurts.** Recognize when there's a mismatch between a team member's personal values, morals, and principles and your organization's values, morals, and principles. Not every situation will be as cut-and-dry as a person acting immorally or unethically, and weeding them out may appear to be as controversial as their actions. Regardless, effective leaders are responsible for progressing their organization's vision, maintaining synergy amongst team members, and developing individuals. That will often require you to make hard decisions.

Principle #11 in Action

Kobe Bryant and Shaquille O'Neal (Shaq) formed one of the most dominant duos in NBA history! They terrorized defenses with their combination of maneuverability across the court and dominance on the inside, and they capitalized on their dominance by winning three of their four NBA Finals appearances. Despite their success, the Lakers made the bold decision to trade Shaq in 2004—just after their fourth Finals appearance. Why? Leadership decisions often require balancing talent with team dynamics, and Shaq's off-court behavior and contextual character flaws eventually outweighed his on-court contributions.

- Shaq's lack of conditioning and work ethic contrasted sharply with Kobe's relentless drive. Kobe later reflected, "I wish he was in the gym. I would have had twelve [expletive] rings." Shaq's unwillingness to prioritize fitness or off-season preparation frustrated teammates and coaches.
- Shaq's public feuds with Kobe and the Lakers management undermined team unity. He once yelled, "Pay me!" at owner Jerry Buss during a preseason game, and his constant jabs at Kobe through the media strained their partnership.
- While Shaq's charisma made him a locker room favorite and marketing icon, his focus on acting, music, and endorsements during the season often distracted him from basketball. His leadership style, reliant on humor and charisma, clashed with Kobe's disciplined approach, and Shaq's dismissive attitude toward criticism alienated others in the organization.

The decision to trade Shaq wasn't easy—he was still a dominant force, as shown by his 2006 championship with the Miami Heat. Yet, effective leaders must sometimes make difficult choices to align their team's values, vision, and synergy. The Lakers recognized that Shaq's values and principles no longer aligned with their organizational goals, and his presence risked undermining team progress.

Initially, the trade seemed costly, with the Lakers enduring a losing season in 2004–2005 and being eliminated in the first round of the playoffs the following two seasons. However, by focusing on building around Kobe and maintaining team cohesion, they won two of their next three Finals appearances. This move reinforced the principle that leaders must prioritize their organization's vision, even when it means making painful decisions that may cause short-term setbacks.*

The Last Word on Principle #11

- Which performance gaps on your team are clearly skills or knowledge gaps you can train for?
- What observable behaviors would you classify as character issues rather than fixable skill deficits?

---

* Disclaimer: I'm a huge Shaq fan! This isn't a jab at him, a swipe at his legacy, or an endorsement of the Lakers' management decisions. Instead, it's an example of a situation that's not as conclusive as one in which the team member does things that are morally and ethically wrong. Shaq—a Naismith Memorial Basketball Hall of Fame inductee—was a phenomenally talented player and a giant in the community (pun intended). Yet, his values did not align with team values, ultimately ending with the Lakers weeding him out so the team could grow. Not all situations are cut-and-dry, but our obligation to lead effectively remains.

- What is your step-by-step process for coaching a training issue from diagnosis to follow-up?
- How will you document and escalate persistent character concerns so they're handled fairly and consistently?

PRINCIPLE #12

BUILD EACH OTHER UP

Encouragement begets engagement.
Engagement produces results.

I emphasized weeding people out in the last principle, because that's where we often struggle the most; however, many of us are well meaning but inconsistent in nurturing growth through encouragement. So, what else can we do to positively influence our team members and leave a lasting impact on their lives? Susan Page states in her book *The Power of Business Process Improvement* that, "*Impact* refers to the effect that the business process has on the organization" (2019). Many leaders, including me, study books like this to develop tangible processes that will impact the organization's bottom line. In doing so, we sometimes fail to recognize the impact of building each other up. I understand why: Simply telling people how awesome they are won't do much aside from transform the workplace into a glorified cheer camp. Instead, we must create an environment where encouragement isn't just rhetoric but a strategic action that enhances performance and drives business success.

Let's mix it up in this section. We will combine the **Implementing Principle #12** section with **Principle #12 in Action** using Susan Page's steps as the framework and our favorite manager, Sarah, as the example. Using Page's framework will allow us to create a supportive and encouraging environment that produces measurable results. Let's dive in!

> **Tip:** Read *The Power of Business Process Improvement* for additional context and actionable steps to improve *all* business processes.

How to Put Principle #12 in Action

10 Simple Steps to Build an Encouraging Environment (Adapted from Susan Page's *The Power of Business Process Improvement*)

1. **Create a process inventory.** Identify key team members' strengths and areas where they need support. This is where you will focus your time and efforts.

    a. Example: Sarah called Lisa into her office and pulled out her *Nurturing Growth Cheat Sheet.* "Let's discuss your skills. From your perspective, what are you good at and where do you need improvement? What do you contribute to the team?" Sarah started. This skills audit will uncover hidden talents and opportunities for professional growth.

2. **Establish the foundation.** What is the end goal for each team member? What are you encouraging him or her to do? Define each team member's goals and align them with organizational goals.

    a. Example: Sarah continues in her meeting with Lisa, "What are your professional goals, and how do you think they align with the company's goals?" Now that Sarah understands Lisa's skills and goals, she can effectively communicate how Lisa's contributions impact the overall mission, making Lisa feel valued as she gains a better insight into how she fits into the overall picture. This is a perfect opportunity for Sarah to set or reaffirm clear boundaries, ensuring professionalism, fostering mutual respect, and preventing misunderstandings that could undermine trust or team dynamics.

3. **Draw the process map.** Map out how team dynamics flow, identifying interactions where encouragement and collaboration are most critical. Define activities, potential problem areas, and how you will measure impact.

    a. Example: Sarah stands up and writes "experiential learning" and "leadership development" on her whiteboard and assigns Lisa's next "stretch" assignment. Additionally, Sarah discusses the resources Lisa has at her disposal and what authorities she has with this new assignment. Sarah didn't stop there; she drew out how this assignment mutually supports parallel efforts and identified early friction points and collaborative opportunities with other team leads in the organization.

4. **Estimate the time and cost.** Every action in business comes at a cost. Understand the time and resources required to build a supportive culture.

    a. Example: Sarah can already tell that this stretch assignment is starting to overwhelm Lisa, so she says, "Don't worry. I've asked Ben to mentor you through the early stages to get this project off to a good start. You'll also check in with me twice a week to provide status updates until you move to Phase 2 of the project. Then, we will transition to biweekly check-ins."

       Sarah is allocating time for one-on-one check-ins, mentoring, and professional development sessions. Additionally, she's assigning Ben, a team lead with twelve years of experience, as a mentor. Peer-to-peer mentorship is an effective tool for building a supportive environment, but ensure that the people you assign as mentors are capable of maintaining their own workload while guiding your team members. Maintain open lines of communication with the mentor and mentee, and be aware of when to step in to avoid the perception that you have delegated the time and costs to someone else. Overall, don't underestimate the costs associated with supporting team members.

5. **Verify the process map.** Validate the accuracy of your understanding of team dynamics by seeking feedback from your team members.

   a. Example: As the project continues, Sarah regularly asks Lisa, "Do you feel supported and heard?" during her check-ins. Lisa initially felt like this was a strange question, but quickly realized that this was her opportunity to ask for additional resources, authorities, and guidance. Sarah realized this was her chance to gather objective insights while still acknowledging Lisa's progress or lack thereof. Here are some sample questions you can ask during this step:

      i. Do you feel you have the resources, guidance, and support needed to achieve your goals? If not, what specific areas could we improve?
      ii. Are there any obstacles in your work environment or processes that hinder your ability to perform effectively?
      iii. What are your thoughts on the level of communication and collaboration within the team? Are there specific ways we can make it more effective?
      iv. Do you believe your contributions are valued and recognized? Can you share an example of when you felt supported or unsupported?

6. **Apply improvement techniques.** Implement strategies to build others up. Strategies like recognition programs or collaborative goal-setting go a long way.

   a. Example: Sarah notices that Lisa's team is doing well on the stretch assignment, so she starts to highlight Lisa's work in meetings and with other managers. Be as creative as your organization or industry allows to highlight accomplishments. For example, I've seen many leaders use LinkedIn to showcase the talent of their team by highlighting how their actions contribute to the organization and the industry as a whole.

7. **Create internal controls, tools, and metrics.** Develop tools to simplify the process and make it a natural part of your team's daily dynamics. Measure the impact of encouragement on team morale and performance.

   a. Example: Sarah has been doing this for a while, so she knows that her interactions with Lisa can't be in a silo. She must provide the same guidance, mentorship, and encouragement to all her team members. Then, she's able to track key metrics, such as engagement scores, retention rates, and productivity improvements. Sarah reviews annual surveys, exit interviews, voluntary turnover rate data, and employee Net Promoter Scores (e.g., "How likely are you to recommend X Organization to others?") to assess whether her supportive leadership is effective.

8. **Test and rework.** Regularly assess whether your approach to building others up is effective, efficient, and adaptable. Make the necessary adjustments based on this assessment.

    a. Example: Alongside her regular one-on-one sessions, Sarah leads quarterly feedback sessions to identify what's working and what's not. She asks her team directly, "What needs to change? Why? Who's impacted? What are the political potholes—the subtle or overt obstacles created by interpersonal conflicts, hidden agendas, or power dynamics that can disrupt collaboration and hinder progress?"

9. **Implement change.** Record strategies and practices that successfully foster a culture of encouragement. Use this data to develop or refine your team's change management process. Additionally, consider how you are teaching your subordinate leaders to implement this change.

    a. Example: Sarah uses the feedback from Lisa and her peers to create a playbook that they and other leaders can use to empower their teams.

10. **Drive continuous improvement.** Plan for the future. Sustain the improvement and keep pace with changing environments by continuing the cycle of evaluation, testing, assessment, and execution. Solicit organizational support for fostering a culture of building others up.

a. Example: Sarah concludes her quarterly leadership meetings with something she terms "Botched and Knocked," where she shares areas where the team didn't perform well (botched) and celebrates wins ("*knocked* out of the park"). She then shares the success data with her supervisors to illustrate how encouraging her team has a measurable impact on the organization.

Quick aside: Some of you may be casting doubt on the idea that systemized encouragement can produce quantifiable results. So, let's examine the data: A May 2024 Gallup study titled "The Relationship Between Engagement at Work and Organizational Outcomes" reports that engaged teams outperform their peers. Bottom line: **It works!** See Table 1 for the report's data.

WHAT HIGHLY ENGAGED EMPLOYEES ACHIEVE MORE OF:		WHAT HIGHLY ENGAGED EMPLOYEES ACHIEVE LESS OF:	
10% higher customer loyalty/engagement	23% higher profitability	78% less absenteeism	28% less shrinkage (theft)
14% higher productivity (production records and evaluations)	70% higher well-being (net thriving employees)	21% less turnover for high-turnover organizations	63% fewer safety incidents (accidents)

18% higher productivity (sales)	22% higher organizational citizenship (participation)	51% less turn-over for low-turnover organizations	32% fewer quality defects

Table 1. Comparison of outcomes for highly engaged employees, adapted from Gallup's "The Relationship Between Engagement at Work and Organizational Outcomes" (2024). Data show that engagement drives higher performance, well-being, and organizational citizenship while reducing turnover, absenteeism, and safety incidents.

Source: Source: Harter, J. K., et al. (2024). "The Relationship Between Engagement at Work and Organizational Outcomes": Q12 Meta-Analysis: 11th Edition. Gallup.

The Last Word on Principle #12

- Who on your team could use a public deposit of trust or recognition this week, and what will you say?
- What routine (meeting opener, shout-out, email) will you start to make encouragement systematic, not accidental?
- When have you failed to build someone up, and how will you repair that relationship?
- How will you measure whether your "build up" efforts improve morale or performance over the next month?

PRINCIPLE #13

GIVE YOUR TEAM MEMBERS A VOICE

"Our lives begin to end the day we become silent about the things that matter."

Martin Luther King, Jr.

As you can see, building each other up isn't about compliments and high fives; it's about opening the lines of communication to provide and receive constructive feedback, creating a supportive and productive environment. Research shows that we thrive in these types of environments, because we feel we have a voice. Earlier, we discussed what giving someone a voice is not. Now, let's talk about what it *is*, because no one enjoys being a member of a team when their opinions and ideas aren't valued or heard.

Implementing Principle #13:

1. **Actively listen to *understand* your team members' input, not to *respond*.** It's easy to hear or skim another's input; however, active listening takes practice. It requires you to study your verbal cues, tone of voice,

body language, and facial expressions while listening to input. Ask questions, nod along, mirror body language, and share the moment.

2. **Giving everyone a voice ≠ workplace democracy.** Effective leaders allow team members to contribute to important decisions and daily operations. They establish buy-in from their team members by showing them how their voice and efforts contribute to the organization as a whole, without giving the perception that they are in a power-sharing agreement with management. In essence, effective leaders flatten information flow by removing extra layers of complexity while maintaining the integrity of the organization's structure to provide clear roles, authorities, and responsibilities; retain opportunities for career progression; and ensure streamlined decision-making processes.
3. **Encourage well-informed input.** My mom taught us at an early age, "If you don't have anything nice to say, don't say anything at all." This lesson taught us to be considerate about what we say so our words are constructive, not a waste. In the workplace, informed input is constructive input. Encourage your team members to master their craft and gather factual information to give well-informed recommendations.

Principle #13 in Action

Another profound memory I have at Tyson is of a lady receiving what I call a "$10,000 coin." As part of a regular meeting, Donnie would hand out small coins to employees who saved the company money. In one instance, Donnie recognized a lady who saved the company $10,000 that year. For context, Tyson's revenue was over $34 billion that year, making this seem inconsequential. In isolation, that's equivalent to celebrating your child for finding a rusted piece of a penny that was spat out by your lawnmower. However, this lady recognized that she could save the company money by making a minor tweak, so she brought the idea to her supervisors. I can imagine her supervisors were a bit skeptical at first, but they probably concluded, "Hey, what's the harm?" The lady worked through the process of implementing this change, and to her delight, Tyson immediately implemented the change.

I didn't interview the lady, but I assume she didn't recommend this change for the coin, because although the coin is sentimental, it lacks monetary value. Instead, she recognized that everyone plays an essential role in accomplishing the overall mission and used her voice to spark a small change that she believed would have a lasting impact. She knew that her idea aligned with the company's vision to "lean out" or eliminate wasteful processes, so she spoke up.

This lady's bold decision to speak up is a perfect example of how while using your voice may not significantly impact the bottom line, it may create a chain of events that increase individual buy-in across the organization and spark a change.

The Last Word on Principle #13

- When was the last time you truly listened to a team member without planning your response? How might actively listening change the outcome of your next conversation?

- How can you give your team members a meaningful voice without creating confusion over roles or authority?
- Are you encouraging your team to provide informed, constructive input? What steps can you take to help them prepare before speaking up?
- Think of one small change a team member suggested that you may have dismissed. How could acknowledging it differently create buy-in and spark positive results?

PRINCIPLE #14

DIRECT FEEDBACK BEATS GOSSIPING EVERY TIME

Feedback only builds trust when delivered directly. Gossip destroys it.

Giving someone else a voice is important, but understanding who you're leading and knowing how to use *your* voice to give feedback is imperative. It's essential to note that feedback only works if the person receives it directly in a manner they can process. Gossiping undermines that. Whether positive or negative, feedback about a person in their absence is gossip. Words taken out of context can quickly twist the best intentions into misinformation or *misinterpreted* information. The fix is simple: Give direct feedback to the person it's about.

Implementing Principle #14:

1. **Implement the closed-door policy.** Contrary to popular belief, the open-door policy is ineffective. I've blogged about this topic before; the executive summary is that the open-door policy leads to inefficiencies, degradation

of trust, and inconsistent information flow. The latter two are usually the culprits when it comes to gossiping in the workplace—especially with less experienced leaders. An abundance of unstructured, informal interactions often leads to unfiltered moments where we could easily discuss matters that would otherwise be preserved in our minds. The people you lead trust that you will tell them when there's something they can improve upon. All it takes is for someone to walk by one time and overhear you discussing a team member who is not around for them to begin losing trust in your willingness and ability to remain trustworthy and objective in your evaluations.

2. **Structure your feedback.** Don't let your message get lost in the delivery. This is a double entendre. On one hand, we have to clearly articulate information to the recipient. Be concise, specific, and professional with your words. On the other hand, we have to intentionally choose how we communicate with the recipient. Choose direct communication whenever possible. Refrain from giving public constructive feedback to a person unless the situation calls for it (e.g., a "murder board" or "scrub-down" where a group of people critically examine a proposal, idea, or plan, often asking tough questions to identify potential flaws and weaknesses before moving forward). Refuse to give feedback about a person (or a person's idea) when they aren't around.

3. **Avoid mentioning anyone else unless they are present.** I cannot harp on this enough. In the Marine Corps, there's

a tongue-in-cheek joke: If someone mentions their family, someone might say, "Did the Marine Corps issue you that family?" The point is that anything not "issued" isn't needed for the mission. It's absurd, and most Marines laugh it off now, but when I repeated it about a colleague, he heard it secondhand. Out of context, it felt personal to him instead of playful, and it damaged trust. We discussed and rectified the issue, but that served as a great reminder of why we should avoid discussing others in their absence. It often leads to misunderstandings, which, at best, costs time as we rectify and clarify the situation, and at worst, degrades trust, destroys synergy, and halts your team's progress.

Principle #14 in Action

I watched a short clip on the Oprah Winfrey Network called "The Truth about Gossip." This five-minute clip provides an illustrative example of the detrimental effects of gossip as a guest named Carrie shares her experience of betrayal by a longtime friend who disclosed her deepest secrets to others. This breach of trust led to significant emotional distress and highlighted the destructive impact gossip can have on relationships. Iyanla Vanzant, a life coach and spiritual teacher, discussed the situation with Carrie, emphasizing the importance of direct communication and the harm gossip inflicts on trust and intimacy. Iyanla and Oprah then presented three reasons for gossip: It's accepted, we don't understand the power of our own words, and it diverts attention from our flaws.

This real-life scenario underscores Principle #14. Engaging in gossip, even with seemingly good intentions, can lead to misunderstandings, erode trust, and damage relationships. Conversely, addressing issues directly with the person involved fosters transparency, builds stronger connections, and prevents the negative consequences associated with indirect communication.

- Don't gossip or excuse it as an inevitable part of human nature.
- Don't underestimate the power your words have and the impact they will have on team dynamics.
- Don't use gossip to deflect or distract others from seeing your inadequacies.
- Eradicate all signs of gossip.

The Last Word on Principle #14

- How does each person on your team prefer to receive corrective feedback (private, public with praise first, written follow-up, etc.)?
- Who will you give direct, constructive feedback to this week instead of talking about them behind their back?
- What rule or routine will you introduce to stop gossip (e.g., closed-door policy, "feedback first" protocol)?
- How will you respond when you hear gossip, so the behavior is corrected without escalating drama?

The Ripple Effect

As you can see, leadership is about more than just managing people—it's about shaping the environment they operate in. As you reflect on the principles in Part 2, consider this: Every decision, word, and action contributes to the culture you're creating. You're not just resolving workplace issues and making people happy by eradicating gossip, weeding out those who don't fit, or giving your team members a voice; you're cultivating trust and strengthening relationships. You're applying *all* of these principles to create an environment where your team can thrive.

Building a healthy culture is no accident; it's a deliberate, creative process. And that's where we begin in Part 3.

PART 3

HOW ARE YOU LEADING? INFLUENCING THE CULTURE

"Bro, how did he do that?" I asked my wife. "There's no way!" That was my genuine reaction to Reza, "The World's Top Touring Illusionist." I was captivated by a performer who openly admitted that his acts were illusions. Yet there I was, paying to watch him pretend to levitate, guess the impossible, and regenerate half-eaten Oreos.

What fascinated me wasn't just the tricks—it was how Reza, an ordinary man with extraordinary talent, used creativity to influence perception. Despite knowing it was an illusion, I still believed in the moment. That's the power of creativity and innovation.

The Reza Effect

Leaders can learn a lot from Reza. Like him, we aim to inspire, not manipulate—to create environments where others believe in the impossible and achieve amazing things. My favorite part of Reza's act wasn't the tricks—it was when he shared how an illusionist had inspired him as a child. He then brought a young child on stage, taught him a trick, and gave him tools to try his illusions.

With every show, Reza isn't just entertaining—he's influencing a *culture* of self-starters and creatives. As leaders, we have the power to do the same by creating environments where innovation, growth, and belief in potential thrive.

What Is Culture?

Culture is a term we hear often, but what does it mean in the context of leadership? *Forbes* defines *workplace culture* as "the shared values, belief systems, attitudes, and assumptions that people in a workplace share" (Agarwal 2018). Prolific leaders like Urban Meyer have encapsulated its importance with quotes like, "Leaders create culture. Culture drives behavior. Behavior produces results" (Meyer and Coffey 2015).

However, creating or influencing culture often feels abstract and elusive. For clarity, let's look to biology, where *culture* is defined as "maintaining conditions suitable for growth." This definition gives us a practical framework: As leaders, our role is to establish shared values and create environments where individuals and teams can grow.

The Fundamentals

To influence culture effectively, leaders must focus on key fundamentals:

- **Exercise self-awareness and self-control.** Toxic leaders often underestimate the impact of their actions on others.
- **Be respectable before demanding respect.** True respect is earned through character and actions, not titles or positions.
- **Hold firm to your beliefs and values.** Leaders like Malcolm X and Walt Disney overcame incredible odds by staying true to their ideals.
- **Start with your own house.** Before seeking external solutions, focus on improving internal processes and leveraging employee-generated solutions.
- **Lead by example.** Actions speak louder than words; align your behavior with your principles to build trust and credibility.

These fundamentals provide the foundation for creating "conditions suitable for growth." Now, let's explore how to achieve the Reza effect and influence culture through creativity, innovation, and effective leadership the final seven principles.

PRINCIPLE #15

MEET PROBLEMS HEAD-ON

Problems are unavoidable,
so prepare to deal with them.

You *will* encounter problems in the workplace. How you address those problems determines the environment you're creating for those you lead. Many leaders leave problems unresolved for three reasons: (1) They don't know about them due to poor information flow, (2) they dislike or fear confrontation, and/or (3) they don't take ownership of the problem.

Let's discuss.

Implementing Principle #15:

1. **Hunt for problems and inefficiencies.** Some of the best advice I received as a young leader was, "Just because you don't see it doesn't mean it's not happening." I eventually learned that if I don't see a problem, it's because I haven't flattened communication flow.

Instead, I've hidden behind a bureaucratic process that covers problems under layers of excuses and secrecy. Use and encourage clear, concise language when discussing problems, establish a psychologically safe space for your team members, and expeditiously address problems.

2. **Don't delegate or shy away from hard conversations.** "They're going to kill each other!" That's the call my parents received many times when my brothers and I were out playing basketball—only to see us laughing and having a good time once they arrived. We obviously weren't masters of conflict resolution based upon the initial call; however, those clashes with my brothers taught me to never fear confrontation or back down from a challenge. Establish mutual respect with each team member, so you can normalize constructive conflict. You'll do this by framing disagreements as *opportunities for growth* and better decision-making. Don't allow the battering-ram technique the Ogunyemi brothers used in their youth; teach your team active listening, deescalation, and negotiation.

3. **If you can influence it, it's your problem.** Don't be the leader who retains all credit and passes problems and issues off to the organization or "system." Leadership positions often come with authority, meaning you have a certain level of influence. The longer you're with the organization, the more you become a part of the "system" you blame issues on. One of my mentors once told me, "Don't waste your seat at the [decision-making]

table." In other words, take ownership and be a part of the organization's progression and solutions to problems.

Principle #15 in Action

I find inspiration for my Principles in Action everywhere I look (if you haven't noticed by now). For example, let's review how SpongeBob SquarePants met a problem head-on in the episode "Graveyard Shift." Yes, you read that right . . . We're about to discuss SpongeBob in a leadership book.

Brief Summary of the Episode

Mr. Krabs tasks SpongeBob and Squidward with running the Krusty Krab during the graveyard shift. SpongeBob becomes increasingly paranoid as the night goes on after hearing Squidward's made-up story about the Hash-Slinging Slasher. Squidward continues to fan the flames of panic instead of addressing the issue of their fear and finding a rational solution, thus escalating the problem.

Eventually, SpongeBob decides to confront his fear directly. SpongeBob takes a proactive approach by preparing himself to face the Hash-Slinging Slasher head-on, even when strange events occur (like flickering lights and mysterious phone calls). Ultimately, the problem is resolved when the mysterious figure turns out to be a harmless, confused fish looking for a job.

How does this episode relate to Principle #15?

1. **Hunt for problems and inefficiencies:** SpongeBob's initial reaction is rooted in fear and poor communication,

but he eventually flattens the information flow by investigating what's happening instead of relying on secondhand exaggerations from Squidward.

2. **Don't shy away from hard conversations:** While Squidward avoids responsibility and feeds into the chaos, SpongeBob faces his fears directly by preparing to engage the supposed slasher instead of running away or ignoring the situation.
3. **If you can influence it, it's your problem:** SpongeBob understands that he has a responsibility to protect the Krusty Krab as an employee—even if it means confronting the unknown. SpongeBob takes ownership of the situation instead of passing off the issue or waiting for Mr. Krabs to handle it.

This was a humorous example, but like SpongeBob, we often face challenges. SpongeBob's challenges were created and exacerbated by misinformation. Where do your challenges come from?

We cannot allow fear, misinformation, or similar to dictate our actions. Effective leaders maintain control, resolve issues, and create a culture of confidence and accountability by meeting problems head-on . . . the SpongeBob way.

Quick aside: I'm sure some of you chuckled when you read that I was about to use SpongeBob as an example. Others, particularly some of my executive readers, may have felt a little skeptical, especially after I used another cartoon reference earlier in the book. This is the perfect place to explain why I include these pop culture references.

This book is built around *counterintuitive* principles for leaders.

In this principle, I'm encouraging you to ***hunt*** for inefficiencies, which means becoming comfortable looking at old problems in new ways, from different perspectives. At the risk of alienating some readers or being perceived as less professional, these references serve as a reminder that implementing principles like facing problems head-on isn't always straightforward. Leading people in complex work environments requires creativity, finding new ways to articulate the mission, and influencing behavior to leave a lasting impact.

Hopefully, these pop culture references will resonate and help the point sink in. At a minimum, I hope this explanation transforms the book from a frisbee you toss across the room into a boomerang—something you can keep coming back to, enjoy, and learn from.

The Last Word on Principle #15

- What current problem have you been avoiding that, if addressed now, would remove a daily friction point for your team?
- What process will you put in place so problems are raised early, not hidden until they become crises?
- How will you model responding to problems in a way that encourages others to bring issues forward?
- What is one small "problem" you can solve this week that will show your team you're serious about tackling issues quickly?

PRINCIPLE #16

HOLD THE LINE

"You will not pass" is more than just a catchy quote.

Meeting problems head-on requires initiative and courage, which enables us to make hard, unpopular decisions despite adversity and condescending opinions. This is what I call *holding the line*. That phrase makes me envision a small but brave unit interlocking shields to prepare for a formidable foe's attack. In this vision, a brave leader stands somewhere in the mix, yelling, "Hold!" as his unified force refuses to give in to the pressure exerted against it. The force's persistence and combined strength allow them to repel the enemy's attack.

That's the kind of leader I'm encouraging you to be—one who maintains their integrity while embodying and reinforcing the company's standards without giving in to peer pressure or cutting corners.

Implementing Principle #16:

1. **Set and maintain clear boundaries to create autonomy.** Many leaders believe that the best growth happens when you create an environment with little to no boundaries. Leaders do this to increase autonomy—full control over work tasks and processes. This claim is supported by research like an article published in *Frontiers of Psychology* that states, "Increased perceived autonomy can significantly improve individual and group productivity" (Johannsen and Zak 2020). However, effective leaders can achieve optimal results by striking a balance between autonomy and structured guidance (boundaries). Ken Blanchard said, "Boundaries have the capacity to channel energy in a specific direction." That means we can help our team members grow by striking a balance between autonomy and boundaries.

   To do so, let's borrow a philosophy from our friends in biology. Ever wonder why plants fail to grow to maturity and die when they start in pots that are too large? It's because the environment is not conducive to developing a healthy root structure. Instead, the person planting should start the plant in a smaller pot (boundaries) and move it to a large pot once the roots grow stronger and the plant matures. Similarly, we should provide clear, regular guidance to our team members to ensure their efforts align with team and organization goals and values. The frequency of and details in your guidance (boundaries) can decrease as the team member demonstrates an increased understanding of the environment and sustained high performance.

2. ~~If you can't beat 'em, join 'em.~~ **If you can't change it, enforce it.** One of the enemies leaders must hold the line against is the slippery slope of selectively enforcing rules. Many leaders, including me, have looked past enforcing "dumb" rules—the ones that don't make sense and may even hamper progress. Enforcing them can make you stand out as a "stickler," so the temptation is to turn a blind eye, blend in, and unintentionally communicate that we only follow *convenient* rules. **That's the real enemy: selective enforcement. It erodes consistency, discipline, and trust.**

    a. **Caterpillar vs. chameleon.** Caterpillars grow in their environment instead of blending in to avoid recognition. A caterpillar embraces its transformative journey and is committed to evolving into something extraordinary while remaining within the boundaries of its environment. Chameleons, on the other hand, adapt by changing colors to fit in, often at the expense of their true identity. **Effective leaders are caterpillars, not chameleons.** They enforce all standards and make the hard, unpopular calls when necessary. Change the standard or enforce it. That's holding the line.

3. **Maximize potential by destroying complacency.** "Elite organizations do not accept mediocrity and they do not

look the other way when teammates come up short of expectations. We must hold each other accountable" (Berger 2019). Complacency often limits potential, as pride in past achievements leads individuals to settle for "good enough." I remember the seething resentment I felt after receiving unexpected C- grades from two influential educators—one in junior high and the other in college. Though I put forth little effort on the projects, I *knew* mine were better than those of the majority of my classmates, yet I received the same grade (or worse) than them. Both teachers had the same response, "You can do better." They both sought to teach me that complacency results from neglecting growth and relying too heavily on natural talent. I got the point after the second time. Effective leaders—like these two educators—address complacent habits by setting individualized goals and maintaining high personal standards. By doing so, they inspire others to break free from mediocrity and foster an environment where team members can achieve their fullest potential.

Principal #16 in Action

Coach Tony Dungy is one of my favorite leaders to study, not just because he is a Hall of Fame Coach, but because his values and principles resonate with me. He exemplified what it means to hold the line by maintaining a steadfast adherence to his philosophy to transform struggling organizations into championship-caliber teams.

When he became the head coach of the Tampa Bay Buccaneers in 1996, Coach Dungy faced a team that had what he described as a "fragile mindset"—often expecting negative results and consequently meeting their expectations. Many in his position would have succumbed to pressure to seek quick fixes. Coach Dungy held the line by focusing on culture, discipline, and long-term growth. He confronted mediocrity directly and set uncompromising standards—even when it meant making unpopular decisions or enduring criticism for the team's initial struggles.

Clear Boundaries Create Culture and Accountability

Coach Dungy revolutionized the Buccaneers by establishing clear boundaries and expectations for his players on and off the field. Many say, "Football is a game of inches," so Coach Dungy refused to allow his team to suffer "death by inches." Accordingly, his philosophy emphasized fundamentals, attention to detail, and doing ordinary things extraordinarily well. These boundaries didn't stifle creativity; they created a framework where players could thrive within a culture of professionalism and respect.

Coach Dungy's approach to leadership reflects Ken Blanchard's assertion: "Boundaries have the capacity to channel energy in a specific direction." Coach Dungy didn't eliminate autonomy—he *earned* his team's loyalty and faithfulness by prioritizing a people-first culture. For example, he fought for his coaches to keep their jobs, even when the team was not winning as many games as the Buccaneers executives believed they should. As a result, players and coaches bought into Coach Dungy's vision, because they knew he cared deeply about their well-being and development.

Addressing Mediocrity to Drive Excellence

The perception could have easily been that Coach Dungy accepted mediocre performance and marginal improvements in his fight to gain his team's loyalty. Contrarily, his unwillingness to tolerate complacency was critical to the Buccaneers' transformation. He confronted underperformance head-on, reinforcing the team's commitment to a shared vision.

This commitment to accountability carried over to his tenure with the Indianapolis Colts, culminating in a Super Bowl victory in 2007. Even after his departure, the culture Dungy instilled endured, proving that holding the line and maintaining high standards had a lasting impact.

Lessons for Today's Leaders

Ultimately, Coach Dungy amassed 148 wins, with only seventy-nine losses throughout his coaching career, and he was enshrined into the Pro Football Hall of Fame in 2016. His successful leadership shows us that holding the line isn't about rigidity or resistance to change—it's about consistency, courage, and creating a culture where excellence becomes the norm. Leaders can inspire their teams to overcome challenges and achieve sustained success by setting clear boundaries, addressing mediocrity, and cultivating loyalty.

Whether you're leading on the field, in the office, or on the battlefield, Coach Dungy's example reminds us that holding the line isn't just a strategy—it's a commitment to integrity and progress.

The Last Word on Principle #16

- Where are you tempted to bend rules or overlook standards? How could consistently holding the line strengthen your team and culture?
- Are you striking the right balance between autonomy and boundaries for your team members? What adjustments could help them grow while staying aligned with your vision?

- When was the last time you addressed complacency—yours or your team's—before it became a habit? How can you proactively challenge mediocrity moving forward?
- Think of a situation where making the hard, unpopular decision could yield long-term success. How can you prepare to stand firm with courage and consistency?

PRINCIPLE #17

PREPARE THE NEXT GENERATION

Leading last is all about leaving a lasting impact.

Like Coach Dungy, we will all leave our current position at some point. The resilience and discipline we exemplify while holding the line sets the groundwork for shaping a culture that leaves a lasting legacy. Oftentimes, our looming rotation date gives us the urge to implement a niche product or process to leave our mark as innovators or change agents. That is admirable, but our goal should instead be to achieve sustainable, long-term success, and the processes, procedures, and documentation we develop should cause longevity.

Implementing Principle #17:

1. **Train the trainer.** We've talked about how effective leaders are studious and how we should establish a continuing education plan for each team member, but let's take it a step further. Our continuing education is often

focused on becoming an individual subject matter expert in a given job—rightfully so. What's missing in a lot of organizations is an effective mentorship program. For example, you're reading this book to become an effective leader, but what's your plan to teach your subordinate leaders these principles? Then, how will you encourage them to teach their team members? And so on. Creating a culture of self-starters is about teaching your team members how to train others and empowering them to develop others. Training the trainer allows you to curate the information being taught across your organization while promoting peer-to-peer learning. This ultimately leads to increased engagement and performance, better employee development, and the establishment of a scalable model where knowledge is continually shared and expanded. Here's the Train the Trainer Cycle Model:

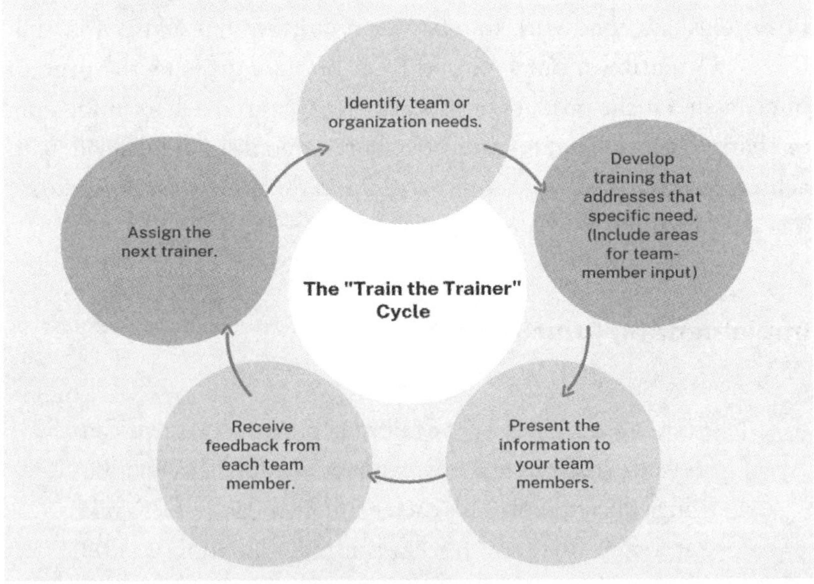

Figure 6. *The Train the Trainer Cycle Model.*

2. **"Establish repeatable processes."** I adopted this phrase from General Austin Miller, the final commander of NATO's Resolute Support Mission and United States Forces—Afghanistan. He repeated this almost daily to: (1) focus our daily actions on developing practices that would sustain after we left, (2) ensure our individual projects and efforts were not too expensive or idiosyncratic to sustain once we left, and (3) encourage us to document successful practices so our successors could implement and build upon our momentum. Effective leaders know how to learn from the past, manage the present, capture best practices, and implement systems that integrate the best of what works with room for innovation. This ensures sustainability while fostering creativity within your team.

3. **"Who's next?"** This phrase is from my favorite World Wrestling Entertainment (WWE) wrestler—the legendary Bill Goldberg! I enjoyed hearing this phrase because Goldberg usually said it after a match. He'd ask, "Who's next to receive my thrashing?!" I'm not challenging you to *thrash* anyone. Instead, I'm challenging you to identify who's next in line to take *your* spot. What are you doing to groom the "future you"? Since effective leaders live for a purpose bigger than themselves, we must make time to mentor and develop individuals who will take our place and achieve greater accomplishments. We invest in ourselves to pour into someone else.

Principle #17 in Action

The WWE has thrived and entertained households for several decades. Its sustained success isn't just about its electrifying performances or global reach; it's about how the organization consistently develops and invests in the next generation of talent. This approach embodies the three critical key insights we discussed that ensure sustainable results: training the trainer, establishing repeatable processes, and grooming future leaders.

1. Train the Trainer: Building a Legacy of Mentorship

The WWE's success is built on a foundation of experienced leaders training the next generation of performers, writers, and producers. Legends like Triple H, Shawn Michaels, and others transitioned from the ring to roles as trainers and mentors, which allowed them to pass on their knowledge of the industry.

Empowering experienced professionals allowed them to teach the nuances of storytelling, branding, and audience engagement. These are critical aspects of the WWE that ensure the traditions and gusto are not lost over time. These trained trainers act as multipliers, creating a ripple effect that enhances the entire organization.

2. Establish Repeatable Processes: Innovation Meets Tradition

WWE thrives because of its ability to blend tried-and-true practices with innovative approaches. Signature events like WrestleMania follow a well-established formula of storytelling, fan engagement, and spectacle while adapting to modern trends like social media campaigns and cinematic-style matches. For perspective, the promotional poster for WrestleMania 1—which took place in March 1985—featured Hulk Hogan and Mr. T. If you don't know who they are, let's just say that their charisma, larger-than-life personalities, dynamic in-ring presence, and promo delivery rivals that of today's Cody Rhodes, Becky Lynch, and Roman Reigns.

The WWE creates repeatable processes that deliver consistent results and encourage experimentation. This has kept fans engaged and invested in the organization. The WWE's ability to remain flexible while adhering to proven successful processes has kept the brand fresh and relevant for decades.

3. Who's Next? Grooming Future Stars

The origin story for Goldberg's iconic phrase is fairly anticlimactic. According to him, he was contemplating his tagline at a restaurant when a waitress said, "Who's next?" He warmed up to the idea and adopted the phrase. The WWE's implementation of "Who's Next?" is much more intentional. The WWE focuses on preparing the next wave of talent with developmental programs like NXT and international recruiting efforts. This organization actively seeks and grooms new stars to carry the brand forward. Investing in these emerging talents and providing them with opportunities to shine ensures continuity and builds anticipation for the future.

Leaders like Vince McMahon and Triple H understand that their legacy depends on the success of those who come after them. The latter is known in recent years for his commitment to nurturing talent. He said, "I want to work with the guys [leaders] who are cultivating talent . . . they're helping them develop and become something more." What's more? "I want each talent to be all that they can be and get to WrestleMania."

What is your team's "WrestleMania?" Perhaps it's a BHAG, a project, or implementing a new technology, training exercise, marketing strategy, or otherwise. Remember: WWE's sustained dominance is a testament to its commitment to training mentors, fostering innovation through structured processes, and grooming the next generation of leaders. Similarly, effective leaders should prioritize creating repeatable processes and a pipeline of future leaders to ensure the longevity and growth of their organization.

Now, ask yourself: "Am I shaping a culture that will prepare the next generation of leaders?"

The Last Word on Principle #17

- Who is "next" on your team—one person you can mentor to take more responsibility in the next six to twelve months?
- What specific skill, process, or value will you teach that person first, and how will you measure progress?
- How will you intentionally create opportunities for that person to lead small projects or decisions?
- What system will you put in place to make mentorship routine (not random) across your team?

PRINCIPLE #18

FOSTER CREATIVITY, INNOVATION, AND RESOURCEFULNESS

Resources may be limited,
but resourcefulness is infinite.

Leaders can benefit from the legacy of those who went before them; however, effective leaders create thriving organizations by integrating fresh ideas and unique perspectives into their tried-and-true systems and processes. Resources include people, skills, finances, tools, equipment, capabilities, and more. An effective leader knows what resources are available to solve any given problem, and they are consistently looking for creative and innovative approaches to problem-solving.

Implementing Principle #18:

1. **Encourage creativity.** Creativity is solving problems **using inventive approaches.** It involves looking at old problems from a new perspective. Begin by being transparent about problems and open to solutions

from your team members. Then, implement some of the following methods to boost creativity:

a. **Create competition.** Competition can bring out the best in people when used appropriately. Teams become stronger and more skilled in the creative process when they engage in healthy competition, because individuals will work to distinguish themselves and their ideas. Challenge your team members to compete with one another to identify areas of growth and motivate better performance. Reward the creative process, not just the results, so your team learns the processes that lead to sustainable success.
b. **Visit other organizations as a team.** Seeing how others solve problems exposes your team to diverse perspectives and fuels creativity.
c. **Talk about something else.** Complex problems sometimes lead to fixation, and fixation causes stagnation. Change the subject. Talk about something else that allows your team to use their imagination. This mental exercise can help shake the feeling of being "stuck" to refresh creative ideas.
d. **Allocate time for brainstorming.** Looming deadlines and deliverables often hamper team members' ability to explore ideas freely. Carve out uninterrupted time and space for the creative process.
e. **Change positions.** Temporarily trading roles or physically changing positions in meetings can give us the perspective shift we need to develop creative ideas.

f. **Fail openly.** Failures are growth opportunities, so your team needs to know that you support them even when they fail—especially when they fail. Failure is part of the creative process.

2. **Encourage Resourcefulness.** Resourcefulness is cleverly **using old tools in new ways** to solve problems. The Marine Corps calls it "doing more with less," meaning, do the best with what you have instead of obsessing over what you don't. Teach your team to use the time, people, funds, and tools (resources) they have at their disposal to accomplish their mission most efficiently. Then, consistently search for resources to enable your team's success and encourage them to do the same.

> Tip: There's a fine line between culturing resourceful leaders and perpetuating an impoverished mindset throughout your organization. An impoverished mindset in this context is a stifling fear of spending budgeted money or taking risks to obtain resources that would help achieve team or organizational goals. In other words, if you *need* a Ferrari and have *budgeted* for a Ferrari, don't waste time modifying a go-kart under the guise of being resourceful. Buy the Ferrari!

3. **Encourage Innovation.** Innovation is changing something established by **using new methods, ideas, or**

products. The driving force behind cultivating an environment of innovation is empowering your team members to make changes where necessary. Openly praise those who take risks to enhance areas that need improvement. Challenge your most creative leaders with the most complex problems and find the resources to enable their success. Provide them with your organization's change management framework. If one doesn't exist, develop one like the example below:

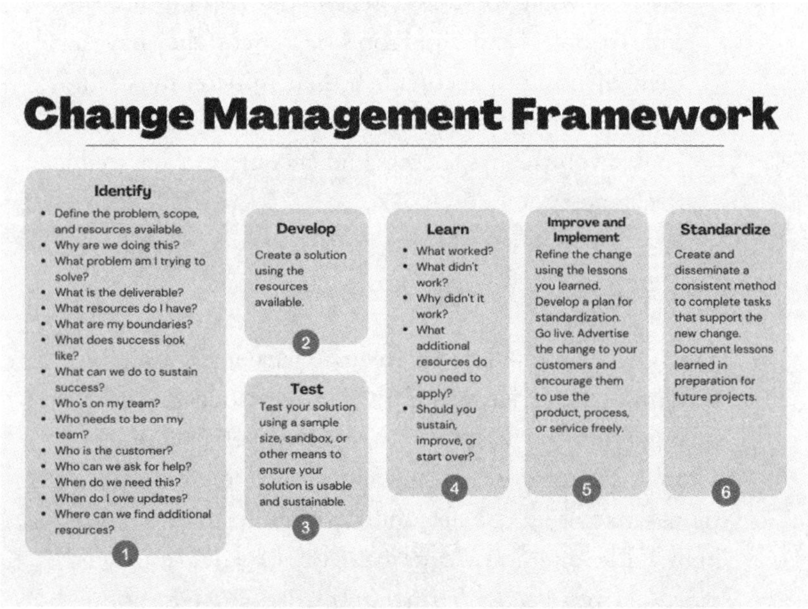

Figure 7. *Change Management Framework.*

Principle #18 in Action

Elon Musk is one of the greatest innovators of our time. You don't have to look far to find one of his Starlink terminals providing high-speed internet around the world, full (supervised) self-driving vehicles that look more like spacecraft than traditional cars and trucks, or reusable rockets—an invention once deemed impossible in the aerospace industry. The latter innovation was a groundbreaking development for SpaceX and serves as a perfect example of how effective leaders can apply Principle #18.

Creativity: Solving Problems with Inventive Approaches

Before SpaceX, the prevailing belief in the aerospace industry was that rockets were single use only, a model that made space exploration prohibitively expensive. Musk challenged this convention by asking his team a simple yet audacious question: "Why can't we land rockets and reuse them?" (Musk communicated the problem.) This led to a BHAG and opened the invitation for creative solutions.

Musk cultivated creativity by pushing his engineers to brainstorm freely, experiment openly, and embrace failure as a learning tool. The team's iterative process included numerous failed attempts—putting the company on the brink of bankruptcy—before they successfully landed a Falcon 9 rocket at Cape Canaveral in 2015. It's important to note that Musk's transparency about SpaceX's failures reinforced the idea that setbacks are part of progress.

Resourcefulness: Doing More with Less

It's easy to discount how resourceful a company like SpaceX is, since it is estimated to operate with a multibillion dollar revenue. However, SpaceX operated on a relatively modest budget in its early days in comparison with aerospace giants with government contracts and vast resources. Musk embraced the Marine Corps' "do more with less" moniker by encouraging his "scrappy little company" to be resourceful. Aside from the fact that they were working to reuse rockets, SpaceX employees repurposed existing technology and developed innovative ways to reduce costs. For example, SpaceX designed and manufactured many rocket components in-house instead of outsourcing parts, which allowed for greater control and significant cost savings. Musk didn't shy away from spending on cutting-edge materials and technology when it aligned with long-term goals. However, he demonstrated the artful balance between resourcefulness and knowing when to invest.

Innovation: Changing the Game with New Methods

Musk's relentless pursuit of innovation at SpaceX transformed the aerospace industry. The Falcon 9's reusability didn't just lower costs—it fundamentally changed the economics of space exploration, enabling missions that were previously unthinkable. Musk's change management framework was evident throughout the process:

1. **Identify:** The problem was clear—the cost of single-use rockets was astronomical.
2. **Develop:** SpaceX engineers worked on reusable rocket technology.
3. **Test:** Early rocket landing attempts were trialed and analyzed, with each failure yielding valuable lessons.
4. **Learn:** Engineers refined the design based on these lessons.
5. **Improve and implement:** The successful landing of Falcon 9 in 2015 set a new industry standard.
6. **Standardize:** At the time of this writing, the Falcon 9 has completed 423 missions, 379 total landings, and 352 total reflights.

By empowering his team to take risks and think beyond the limits of traditional aerospace methods, Musk created an environment where innovation thrived. He encouraged his teams to challenge norms, approach problems with fresh perspectives, use available resources, and take calculated risks while learning from failures. As a result, Musk redefined what humanity thought was possible. Leaders across industries can learn from his ability to cultivate creativity, resourcefulness, and innovation within his teams to achieve groundbreaking results.

The Last Word on Principle #18

- When was the last time you rewarded a well-intentioned idea that failed, and what did you learn from it?
- What one low-risk experiment can your team run this month to try a new approach or tool?
- How will you capture and share the lessons from experiments so the whole team benefits?
- What barriers exist that suppress creative thinking, and what's your first step to remove one of them?

PRINCIPLE #19

DON'T BE LORD OF THE ~~FLIES~~ TASKS

Micromanagement leads to micro-results—and macro frustration.

Effective leaders dream of succeeding and achieving groundbreaking results like SpaceX. We have talented teams with potential, yet we aren't getting the optimized performance and maximum potential we expect. Many of us become anxious and more inclined to hover over our team members, becoming the "lord of the tasks"—one who manages tasks instead of managing people, thereby stifling independent problem-solving. This could create a culture of mistrust, in which your team members believe you have lost trust in their abilities, resulting in chaos, power struggles, and a decline into dysfunction.

The absence of structure and trust can cause team members to provide what you ask for instead of offering the best solution to the problem or the most efficient method to accomplish the task. Team members focus on merely checking boxes and avoiding scrutiny instead of making real progress. It's not rocket science (pun intended); effective leadership requires mastering the balance between clear intent, trust, and verification, ensuring that tasks serve the mission, not just the manager's need for control.

Implementing Principle #19:

1. **Write this down: "The devil is in the details."** Once you've written it down, draw two lines that connect to it as I offer a couple of explanations for this idiom.

    a. The common understanding of this idiom is that **our teams must perform a surgical examination of each problem** or risk overlooking issues that will create complexities in the future. Think of a current problem you're facing or a problem you've faced in the past when you were in charge. Now, underneath one of the lines you drew, write each of your team members' names and consider what unique perspective they bring to the table that can help solve the problem, based on your knowledge of them.
    b. The second explanation of this idiom is that **there's danger in overexplaining and micromanaging *how* a problem is solved.** Underneath the second line, answer the following:

        i. What do I want my team to accomplish?
        ii. What does success look like? (i.e., What conditions need to be met?)
        iii. What boundaries and resources do I need to provide? Allow them to provide feedback on how they'll accomplish the task as you give

regular guidance and refinements based on the information you receive and the current environment.

2. **Build systems to create repeatable processes and foster relationships that yield sustainable results.** Your system is the *means* by which you communicate your intent and receive feedback. The reception of your intent and the quality of your feedback are predicated upon the relationship you have with your team members. Ideally, your team members, especially your direct reports in leadership positions, should reach a point where they can finish your sentences and anticipate your guidance and decisions. This leadership predictability is a result of your transparent leadership and is *essential* for cultivating an environment of self-starters. Consider your primary means (no more than two) for communicating your intent and receiving feedback. For example, you can use in-person team meetings, written memos, or orders to communicate your purpose, and surveys or town hall meetings to gather feedback. When your direct reports make decisions, ask them, "How did you come to that decision?" Their answer, "I did what I thought you would do," or "I made that decision in line with your intent," is usually a good indicator of whether or not you've been transparent and clear in your communication. Figure out what works best for you and your team in your current environment, and apply that approach.

3. **Check yourself before you wreck yourself . . . and your team.** You've probably noticed that this book's constant theme is introspection and connection. That's because it's the beginning of trust, and, according to numerous studies, trust in the workplace drives organizational success. Here are a few questions that you should ask to "check yourself" to know whether or not you're cultivating an environment of self-starters based upon trust:

    a. **Do my team members understand the "why" behind their tasks and decisions?**
        i. Clear intent starts with ensuring your team knows the purpose and big picture, driving their work to empower them to take ownership.
    b. **Am I creating opportunities for team members to make independent decisions?**
        i. Evaluate whether you give them the autonomy to think critically and propose solutions without fear of micromanagement or immediate correction.
    c. **How do my team members respond to challenges or ambiguity?**
        i. Do they freeze and wait for instructions, or do they take the initiative to find solutions aligned with the organization's goals?
    d. **Am I providing consistent, actionable feedback that promotes growth?**
        i. Reflect on whether your feedback fosters confidence and development rather than just

focusing on task completion (i.e., don't be a task lord).

e. **Do I trust my team to make decisions, and do they trust me to support them?**
    i. Trust is a two-way street. Ask if you're empowering your team to lead while maintaining their confidence in your support and guidance.

Principle #19 in Action

Remember Howard Schultz, the successful CEO of Starbucks? Like many of us, he has made some costly mistakes that we can learn from. His early leadership struggles and openness about them align perfectly with Principle #19. Let's discuss "the other side" of Schultz.

As we discussed earlier, Schultz made a bold move to expand the company rapidly in the early days of Starbucks' growth. While the vision was clear, he later admitted that his initial leadership style lacked the balance of clear intent and trust in his team. Schultz was notorious for being overly involved in every detail, micromanaging decisions, and frequently second-guessing his team's capabilities.

One notable failure was during Starbucks' expansion into Chicago in the late 1980s. Schultz pushed for rapid growth in the area, but his inability to delegate and trust his team led to critical missteps, including poor site selection, inconsistent product quality, and lack of staff preparedness. Customers began to associate Starbucks with inconsistency and high prices rather than premium quality, which led to disappointing sales and a damaged brand image.

Schultz later reflected on this failure in his book *Pour Your Heart Into It*: "I failed to listen, to trust the people I hired, and to respect their knowledge. Instead, I micromanaged and ignored their warnings, thinking I knew better" (Schultz 1997).

What Schultz Learned

The experience humbled Schultz and prompted a dramatic shift in his leadership style. He began to focus on the following:

- **Clear intent:** Communicating the company's vision while giving his team more freedom to execute it.
- **Trust before verification:** Hiring talented people and encouraging them to push back. This empowered his team to make decisions without him hovering and to challenge his ideas that were not the best for the organization.
- **Relationships over systems:** Building stronger connections with his team to ensure mutual understanding and alignment.

By embracing transparency and admitting his failures, Schultz eventually earned his team's trust and cultivated an environment where his leaders felt empowered to take initiative. This shift played a significant role in Starbucks' eventual resurgence as a global coffee powerhouse.

The Last Word on Principle #19

- What task do you currently micromanage that you could delegate this week, and to whom will you delegate it?
- What clear guardrails will you set so you can delegate without losing necessary control?

- How will you measure whether giving freedom on that task increases speed, quality, or morale?
- When a team member struggles after delegation, how will you coach them without reverting to micromanagement?

PRINCIPLE #20

IT'S A WORKPLACE, NOT A LOCKER ROOM

"Locker room" dynamics don't build teams; they destroy cohesion and stall progress.

Schultz's significant shift made a difference in the workplace culture, giving his employees what they needed to grow. Effective leaders understand that bold perspective shifts are sometimes required to progress the organization. One such bold shift is transitioning the workplace from a "locker room" to a professional environment.

Males make up the majority of many work environments. This dynamic sometimes gives the impression that we must submit to the stereotypical attributes, behaviors, and conversations associated with men and boys—you know, the conversations that are rife with crude humor, off-color jokes, or inappropriate comments about others, including discussions about women. Survey after survey proves that this behavior can create a hostile or uncomfortable environment, especially for those who don't share the same humor or values. Many organizations have homed in on this kind of behavior and created low tolerance for such conversations and crude humor. However, there are more "locker room" behaviors to look out for to protect your workplace and foster a safe environment for your team.

Implementing Principle #20:

1. **End unhealthy competitive behavior.** I already stressed the importance of healthy competition, but the antithesis to healthy competition is the obsession with dominance, winning, and outperforming others. Excessive competition can undermine collaborative efforts as team members compete to gain an advantage by undercutting one another. Maintain a healthy balance by focusing your team on growing together through competition, rather than solely rewarding individual success with praise and advancement.

2. **Guard against the "Macho Man" effect.** This topic always causes the 1978 song by Village People, "Macho Man," to linger in my mind. Similarly, the effects of a "macho" culture linger. For example, healthy habits like showing vulnerability are seen as a weakness, which causes people to avoid admitting mistakes or asking for help. Look out for and address aggressive posturing, people talking over others, or individuals being disruptive to assert dominance, because when those actions are commonplace, you may be leading a toxic, unreceptive, and partisan culture. This environment discourages open communication and learning opportunities.

3. **Monitor risk-taking and address overconfidence.** Over the years, I've lost count of how many times I've asked or heard one of my friends ask, "You think I can. . .?" before engaging in some high-risk activity without measuring the costs. We want our team members to take bold actions to achieve bold results; however, taking risks without fully considering consequences and being overly confident in decisions will lead to impulsive actions or failure to weigh alternatives effectively. Don't become risk-averse, but teach your team members to take ***calculated*** risks to achieve success.

Principle #20 in Action

One of the most infamous moments that sparked a global debate and ongoing conversation about workplace culture occurred in 2017, when several high-profile executives in the entertainment and business industries were accused of making crude or demeaning remarks in professional settings. Many of these incidents were brushed off as "locker room talk," but they ultimately led to resignations, public apologies, and the collapse of careers. These moments sparked discussions about how words and actions—especially from those in leadership positions—can influence the workplace environment. It highlighted the importance of maintaining a culture where people are treated with respect and professionalism.

What can effective leaders learn from this?

1. **Words mean things.** This is a common phrase in the military, because a leader's language reflects and

influences the workplace culture. Even offhand remarks can have far-reaching consequences.

2. **You set the tone.** Remember: If you can influence it, it's your problem. That means you must take ownership and embody the values you want to see in your team. Establish clear boundaries for acceptable behavior.
3. **Nip it in the bud.** Address inappropriate or out-of-bounds behavior early, before it can bloom into something worse. Be transparent, concise, and direct, leaving no room for ambiguity or confusion. Cultivating an environment for growth requires us to quickly get to the heart of the matter so team members feel safe and respected in the workplace.

Leaders can avoid the pitfalls of "locker room" dynamics and create environments where all team members thrive by committing to a culture of respect and professionalism.

The Last Word on Principle #20

- Which "locker room" behaviors (language, jokes, side conversations) show up in your team, and how do they affect others?
- What explicit norms will you establish and communicate to prevent those dynamics?
- How will you handle a first instance of boundary-crossing so it's corrective, not shaming?
- What training or conversation should you schedule to create shared understanding of professional conduct?

PRINCIPLE #21

YOU'RE LEADING HUMANS *AND* "ROBOTS"

Tools evolve, but leading with emotional intelligence remains timeless.

Creating an environment where *all* team members can thrive is predicated upon our ability to understand the team members we lead. This book is centered on leading people, because humans cannot be replicated or replaced. Nevertheless, today's technology is indispensable in achieving success. From automating supply chains to developing products, to generating innovative ideas, technology has transformed how we work and solve problems. Effective leaders must excel in guiding both humans, with our emotions and complexities, and "robots," with their efficiency and precision. The challenge is cultivating an environment where technology supplements human ingenuity instead of overshadowing it.

Effective leaders have to be emotionally intelligent enough to understand the impact technology has on their team members. Many people's perception is that "robots," or advancements in technology, will continue to decrease available jobs. The advancement of technology over the past two decades has profoundly transformed the job market, presenting both opportunities and challenges. The rise of AI, cloud computing, e-commerce, and social media has created entirely new industries, resulting in an estimated ninety-seven million new roles, according to a report by the World Economic Forum. That seems like great news when taken out of context. Contextually, that same report estimates that advanced technology will displace eighty-five million jobs.

Okay, there's a positive delta of twelve million jobs. What's the big deal? Shouldn't people just get with the times or get left behind?

The truth is the integration of advanced technology and automation in certain industries (e.g., manufacturing) has disproportionately impacted employment, particularly affecting production and line workers. According to a report by Frank-Jürgen Richter, the "adoption of robotization" has led to 2.25 million robots displacing 1.7 million manufacturing jobs worldwide over the past two decades.

What strategies can effective leaders employ to address the challenges posed by technological advancements?

Implementing Principle #21:

1. **Ethical use—stay within bounds.** Familiarize yourself with your industry's standards and the guidelines for using technology. Ensure that your team's use of technology aligns with your industry's ethical standards and regulations, and regularly review your practices to ensure ongoing compliance. For example, artificial intelligence has taken the world by storm, and many organizations have used it to improve productivity. Even so, its use should not come at the expense of data privacy or transparency.

2. **Maximize technology to supplement, not replace.** Develop strong systems and processes before integrating technology. Technology enhances preexisting systems, but it won't be as effective if no such system is in place. You can use technology to address the inefficiencies you hunted for in Principle #15. An example could be automating repetitive tasks or improving data accuracy while maintaining oversight to ensure quality.
3. **Balance automation with human oversight.** Human intervention and interaction are required to implement technology. It's critical for strategy, decision-making, and problem-solving. That means you have to dedicate resources and will incur risks, which can introduce human error. Don't overlook the costs associated with using technology. Instead, allocate resources to train team members on managing and optimizing these tools, and remain vigilant about risks such as overreliance on automation.
4. **Retrain your workforce.** As the demand for advanced technology increases, so does the requirement to train employees on how to implement this technology. Develop training programs that help workers adapt to new technologies and allow employees to transition into roles focused on operating and maintaining automated systems.
5. **Consider implementing collaborative robotics ("co-bots").** Many companies are adopting "co-bots"—robots intended for direct human-robot interaction within a shared space—allowing robots to handle repetitive tasks while enabling employees to focus on

more complex responsibilities. You may have been fascinated by a similar concept at Sam's Club, where they introduced an autonomous robot that cleans, collects inventory information, verifies pricing, and more. "Our initial goal at Sam's Club was to convert time historically spent on scrubbers to more member-focused activities . . . These scrubbers help associates ensure products are out for sale, priced correctly, and findable, ultimately making it easier to directly engage with our members," said Todd Garner, Vice President, In-Club Product Management. Implementing collaborative efforts like these aims to enhance productivity without significant workforce reductions.

6. **Lead with transparency.** While interning at Tyson Foods, I was once responsible for collecting information on old databases. My job was simple: call people to see how they were using databases that appeared to be outdated. I was shocked by some of the aggressive responses I received—even for databases that hadn't been touched in ten years! That's when I learned that effective leaders must communicate openly about how technological changes will impact employees, customers, and stakeholders. This drastically reduces uncertainty and unnecessary resistance to pursuing the opportunities that emerge from technological advancements.

While technological advancements have created immense opportunities for economic growth, innovation, and job creation, they have also necessitated continuous reskilling and adaptation. Effective leaders must navigate these changes by preparing their teams for a rapidly evolving workplace. This evolution creates an almost magical environment where creativity abounds.

Principle #21 in Action

Let's talk more about Reza, the renowned illusionist. I would've been fascinated if he had guessed which card I was thinking of or knew how many fingers I was holding behind my back, but his show was much more than that—it was an unforgettable experience! He effectively integrates modern technology into his performances to create a captivating and immersive experience for his audiences. His show, Edge of Illusion, includes "concert-level lighting and video production" to create a "one-of-a-kind experience for the entire family!" This fusion of high-tech lighting and state-of-the-art production delivers an almost action-movie-esque atmosphere, which enhances the overall impact of his illusions.

Reza incorporates masterful comedic timing and numerous interactive and inspirational moments, which allowed me (and the others in attendance) the opportunity to experience the magic firsthand. His performances feature illusions such as passing through the spinning blades of an industrial fan and the appearance of a real helicopter, live on stage (yes, you read that right). This showcases his ability to blend traditional magic with modern technological advancements.

Reza enhances the visual and sensory aspects of his shows and sets a new standard for modern illusionists by embracing today's technology. Ultimately, he demonstrates how leaders can harness technology to elevate performance in their workplace and cultivate an environment of success.

The Last Word on Principle #21

- What tool or automation on your team is currently creating friction rather than saving time, and how will you evaluate it?
- How will you ensure that implementing technology also includes a plan for human oversight and emotional impact?
- What is one process you can automate to free up people for higher-value human work this quarter?
- How will you measure whether the human side of your work (trust, judgment, creativity) is improving or declining as you add more tech?

Bringing It All Together

Reza's ability to seamlessly blend technology with creativity and human connection offers a powerful example of modern leadership. He doesn't allow today's pizazz to overshadow his performances. Instead, he enhances the audience's experience and reinforces the timeless wonder of influencing others. His work serves as a reminder that there's no substitute for human ingenuity and emotional connection.

Dr. Martin Luther King Jr. intuitively knew this. He demonstrated that leadership transcends tools and tactics and that it's rooted in understanding, inspiring, and empowering others. Though he lived in a time far removed from today's technological advancements, his ability to connect with people on an emotional and moral level remains a timeless example of how to lead humans effectively. His leadership in the Civil Rights Movement wasn't rooted in commands or coercion, but in understanding the emotions, motives, and struggles of the people he sought to inspire. Dr. King's ability to connect with the humanity of his followers and opponents alike made him one of the most impactful leaders in history.

Dr. King's iconic "I Have a Dream" speech didn't just outline goals; it painted a vivid picture of hope, equality, and unity. By appealing to shared values and the universal desire for freedom and justice, he motivated people from all walks of life to join the movement. Dr. King's leadership was rooted in understanding his followers' aspirations and showing them how their actions contributed to a greater mission.

Dr. King understood that mistakes and setbacks were inevitable in a movement as complex as the fight for civil rights. For example, during the Montgomery bus boycott, logistical missteps and disagreements arose among organizers. Instead of condemning errors, Dr. King used them as opportunities to learn and refine strategies, building a stronger and more resilient movement.

In the face of violence, threats, and relentless opposition, Dr. King provided unwavering emotional support to his followers. He often encouraged nonviolence and forgiveness, even when anger and despair seemed justified. His words and actions reassured his followers that they were not alone, creating a culture of solidarity and emotional resilience. Like an illusionist, Dr. King reshaped what people believed was possible. But unlike an illusion, his impact was real, undeniable, and lasting.

FINAL THOUGHT

"Leadership is the art of getting someone else to do something you want done because he wants to do it."

Dwight D. Eisenhower

You Have a Dream!

You picked up this book because you had a vision. Like me, you imagine yourself influencing millions of people. The thought is exciting and intimidating, so you grabbed this book to learn the secrets to becoming an effective leader. You now have the tools! Hopefully, you take what you learned and apply it to become one of the greatest leaders this world has ever seen.

As leaders in an ever-evolving world, we are called to wield creative tools like Reza, study like General "Mad Dog" Mattis, consult others like Howard Schultz, show empathy like Satya Nadella, and have a vision and unwavering commitment to shared values like Dr. King. We are heroes like Captain Planet when we harmonize these elements to create an environment where our team members thrive, achieving extraordinary results that leave a lasting impact on future generations.

I'm excited to learn about your journey and see how far you go. From now on, you'll connect with your inner self and the humanity of those you lead. By doing so, you will create a culture of trust, collaboration, and shared purpose, ensuring that your team thrives even in the face of adversity. You *will* create an impact that lasts!

EPILOGUE

You Are Qualified

I've had the pleasure of working with numerous brands and participating in various interviews and podcasts. Each interview has challenged me to step outside of where I'm comfortable and share things that I sometimes prefer to keep to myself. Nevertheless, I do my best to be open and honest, so listeners can be inspired by my story and decide to pursue their dreams and purpose. Even so, I'm not always prepared for every question.

One question almost stumped me, as it caused me to pause to reflect: "What qualifies you?" Here I was, a 210-pound Marine in fairly decent shape who, seemingly out of the blue, decided to start publishing children's books and advocating for increasing literacy. There are educators, writers, speakers, and literary professionals—including some of my mentors—who can run circles around me! *How do I answer this question? What qualifies me?*

I answered, "There's no manual for raising children, so having the ability to connect and talk about real topics is a must. I've been a father for over ten years and have been passionate about working with children my entire life. I crave the times we can connect! I wanted to create and share something others like me can use to connect with their children to spark teachable and memorable moments."

I felt like I gave an okay answer, but I also knew I didn't present the qualifications and certifications the interviewer was looking for. Imposter syndrome immediately set in. Here I am presenting as an expert and one who is changing lives, but I have no credentials. That's when I remembered something.

I remembered the videos parents sent me as they used my books to have hard conversations with their children. I recalled how *my* children paraded my books around their classrooms and libraries to show their teachers and friends, who were equally impressed. I remembered the young man who stood up during one of my Q & A sessions and tearfully asked me to come to his house to meet his parents and help him write a book. I remembered the young man who was fascinated by my ability to read and wanted to know how he could learn to read like me.

The memories continued until I finally realized that I had to **write** last—meaning my experiences, passion, and purpose prepared me to influence others well before I decided to publish my first book. Learning how to write a children's book and subsequently publishing three books was simply the means to achieve my purpose.

Some credentialed experts know more than me and are much more skilled; however, many people relate to and are inspired by my story in ways those same professionals cannot influence. That means I am qualified to inspire others and pursue my purpose using whatever resources (or means) are available.

Don't Disqualify Yourself

Similarly, you may have laughed, rolled your eyes, reflected, and taken notes as you read this book. In the end, you may finish reading, borrow a quote or two, and place the book on a shelf or in the thrift store box, assuming that you'll never be the effective leader mentioned throughout this book. Don't believe that!

No matter how or where you were born, you are just as qualified as any of the great leaders I mentioned throughout this book. Somebody needs you, and they are waiting for you to lead them. Your words and actions will resonate with them unlike any other.

You obtained the knowledge and you're ready to apply what you've learned to influence your team and leave a lasting impact on their lives. You're ready to embark upon a new journey to refine your leadership abilities and leave an impact on your organization. You've spent time studying, and now you are prepared to lead.

At last, you have finished this book, and it is time for you to lead! Lead well!

APPENDIX

THE LASTING LEADERSHIP TOOLKIT

As you've learned, an essential part of being an effective leader is being a lifelong learner. Accordingly, I reached out to a few of my mentors, including corporate executives, to solicit their thoughts on *Lead Last*. I developed the following tools and frameworks based on those conversations. In other words, **this is what executives and senior leaders thought you should know**, so take note of how you can address these common leadership challenges. The following tools and frameworks are designed to help you apply the twenty-one principles in real time. Think of this as a complementary toolkit to add additional context and explanations for how you can implement these principles. Let's dive in!

Section A: When Principles Clash

You may find that implementing these principles won't always be straightforward, and sometimes, they may clash in execution. How do you navigate those times?

When to Step In vs. When to Coach Through

Principle #15: *Meet Problems Head-On* **and** Principle #19: *Don't Be Lord of the ~~Flies~~ Tasks*

One of the most challenging decisions a leader must make is determining when to personally intervene to resolve a problem and when to coach a team member through it. Use this decision tree to guide your response.

When should I step in?
DECISION TREE

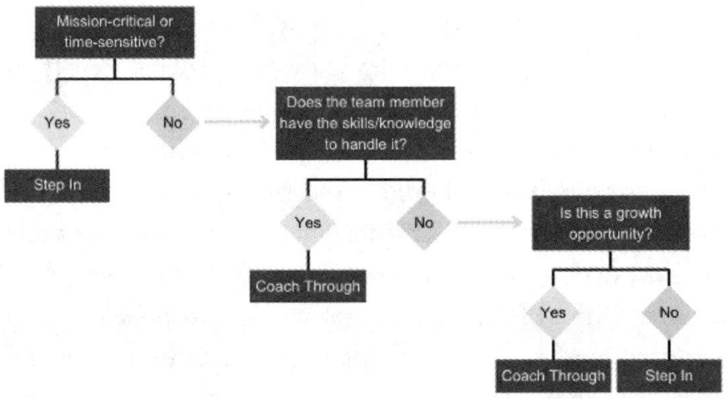

Figure 8. *When should I step in? Decision Tree.*

The Bottom Line: Protect the mission, but don't hinder your team's growth.

Vulnerability vs. Stability

Principle #1: *Let Your Guard Down* **and** Principle #6: *Be Stable and Level-Headed*

We discussed being vulnerable in the workplace, but could revealing your human side make you seem emotionally unstable? When should leaders share their struggles, and when should they remain composed and professional?

Firstly, let's refine our understanding of what vulnerability is in the workplace.

Defining Vulnerability in Leadership

In the workplace, sharing your struggles isn't about unloading emotions or making your team carry your burdens. **It's about transparency, admitting when you've made a mistake, don't have the answer, or need help clarifying the way forward.**

Strategic vulnerability sounds like:

- "Thanks for your feedback. I can see where I was unclear."
- "Team, I was wrong about X."
- "Ladies and gents, I don't have all the answers and am not quite clear on the way forward, so let's spend some time thinking through how we should accomplish this."

Each of these statements acknowledges a gap while reinforcing the importance of collaboration and accountability. Notice that none of them dumps frustration, fear, or insecurity onto the team. That's the difference: **Effective vulnerability creates clarity and trust, not confusion or concern.**

This is why leaders must first grow through their own insecurities. If you haven't done the work of self-awareness and self-regulation, your version of "sharing struggles" may come across as emotional volatility or loss of control. But when you've mastered yourself, you can be transparent in a way that inspires others instead of burdening them.

Alright, let's keep moving.

When should a leader share their thoughts or remain composed?

Here's a simple reference:

- **Share** if: it builds trust, models authenticity, or helps others learn.
- **Stay composed** if: your disclosure shifts the burden onto your team, undercuts confidence in your ability to lead, or is purely self-serving.

The Bottom Line: Vulnerability creates connection, and stability creates trust. Effective leaders balance both.

Direct Feedback Framework

Principle #12: *Build Each Other Up* **and** Principle #14: *Direct Feedback Beats Gossiping Every Time*

Some leaders find it extremely challenging to balance encouraging others while providing direct, corrective feedback. Some ascribe to the "praise sandwich" (i.e., praise-criticism-praise) concept; however, not only is that often ineffective, but it also dilutes the point you are trying to make. By now, you know I love framing my ideas with corny acronyms, so I'll introduce another one to structure your direct feedback without degrading your encouraging environment.

C.L.E.A.R.

- Clarify the situation. "John, I want to talk to you about [situation] because I see potential for you to grow in [area]."
- Lay out facts, not feelings or interpretations. "Here's what I observed. . ."
- Explain the impact. "The reason this is important is because it . . . [explain the effect]"
- Ask for perspective. "What's your perspective on this?" Or a strategy one of my executive mentors uses is, "What did you hear me say?" After they demonstrate they understood, "What do you think about that?"
- Reset expectations. "Alright, let's figure out how to help you excel in this area." This is where you discuss the next steps with a specific timeline.

The Bottom Line: Direct, respectful feedback makes corrections developmental. This allows you to continue to encourage your team members even when they make mistakes.

Section B: The *Lead Last* Leadership Pyramid

I introduced a three-part system, but some of you may be wondering how self-awareness (Principles 1–7) influences learning more about your team and building relationships (Principles 8–14), which enables you to develop a culture of influence (Principles 15–21) and ultimately leave a lasting impact. This theoretical framework is my building block; it demonstrates that before you can leave a lasting effect, you must establish a strong foundation. Here is a visual depiction of what I'm describing:

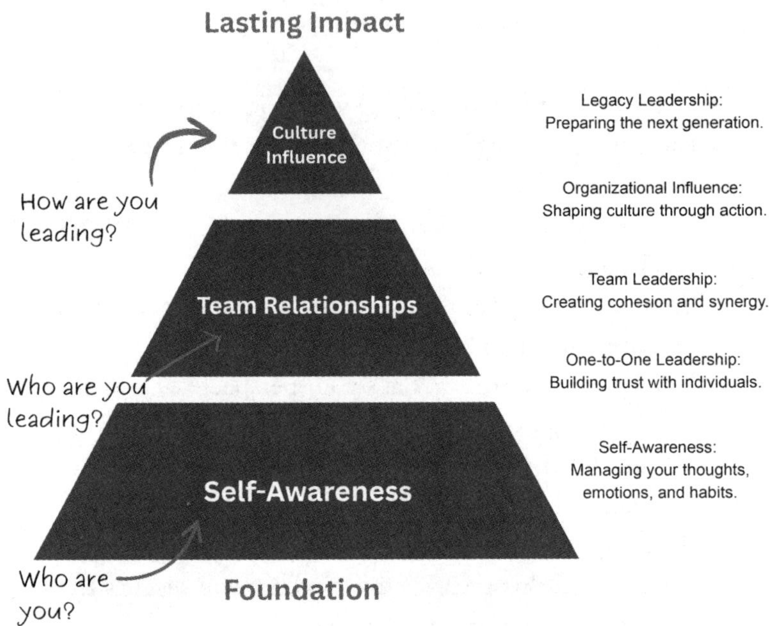

Figure 9. *Lasting Impact Model.*

The Bottom Line: Don't worry, I didn't miss the irony that the concept of *leading last* implies that you are beneath others, elevating them, or behind others, pushing them forward. That would mean that we should use an inverted pyramid, as you've seen in other leadership material. I agree that an inverted pyramid is an excellent depiction of what servant leadership is; however, I didn't develop the *Lead Last* Leadership pyramid to support the hierarchical model. I created it to depict the building block approach to becoming an effective leader. Move up the pyramid with intentionality, without skipping steps.

Section C: A Powerful Case Study

The Real-Life Captain Planet

I read *The Moment of Lift: How Empowering Women Changes the World* by Melinda French Gates after finishing my manuscript, and I was inspired by both the book's message and theme, as well as Melinda's leadership and advocacy efforts over the years, which have had a profound global impact. Melinda exemplified many of the key points we have discussed throughout this book, particularly in building a cohesive team with a diverse range of skills and backgrounds to achieve optimal results.

One of the critical lessons we've covered is that creative and innovative solutions emerge when leaders effectively combine different backgrounds and strengths. Let's look at how Melinda—the real-life Captain Planet—created Captain Planet moments to advocate for women's rights and ignite a global movement.

While coleading the Gates Foundation, Melinda excelled at building teams with diverse experiences, expertise, and backgrounds. She deliberately sought perspectives that weren't naturally represented in their leadership team, often traveling internationally to get the ground truth. The point worth highlighting is that Melinda didn't simply look at the surface-level differences you'd find on a résumé and hope it'd all work out; she created systems to select the right people and ensure different viewpoints shaped decisions.

Example 1: Tackling maternal mortality.

When addressing maternal mortality in developing countries, Melinda didn't rely solely on data from epidemiologists and economists. She insisted on including:

- Local healthcare workers (ground-level operational knowledge)
- Mothers who had experienced the healthcare system (user perspective)
- Community leaders (cultural and social dynamics)
- Policymakers (implementation realities)

Like the Planeteers, each brought a unique "power," but Melinda's brilliance was in creating the framework where these powers could combine. She established decision-making processes that required input from multiple perspectives before major initiatives moved forward.

Example 2: Empowering women through family planning.

Another powerful example from *The Moment of Lift* is Melinda's work on expanding access to family planning resources. She realized that solutions couldn't just come from medical experts or policymakers; they had to include the voices of the women directly impacted. Melinda met with mothers in rural villages who shared their lived experiences, including the barriers they faced when trying to access contraceptives. She paired those voices with the expertise of healthcare providers, economists, and faith leaders who could help shape solutions that were both practical and culturally sensitive. The result was a global initiative that not only allocated resources to communities but also built buy-in, trust, and long-term impact.

One of the most powerful stories within this initiative was the coalitions Melinda helped form to stop police from abusing women and to shift cultural perspectives on family planning in countries around the world. These efforts didn't just change policies; they saved countless lives by reducing the spread of diseases, curbing abuse, and preventing children from being born into situations where their parents couldn't provide care.

This is why I call her the real-life Captain Planet. It's not just because she builds effective teams; it's because she's leveraging those combined powers to save lives across the globe.

The Bottom Line: Captain Planet moments don't happen accidentally. Leaders must intentionally create the conditions for diverse strengths to combine.

Closing Note

Both fictional and real, these Captain Planet moments drive home a simple yet profound truth: Leaders amplify their impact when they intentionally combine diverse strengths toward a shared mission. That's what *leading last* is all about. Whether it's a corporate team aligning strategy and execution or a global foundation saving lives, effective leadership creates conditions where people's powers multiply.

REFERENCES

Agarwal, Dr. Pragya. "How To Create A Positive Workplace Culture." *Forbes*, August 29, 2018. Accessed October 3, 2024. https://www.forbes.com/sites/pragyaagarwaleurope/2018/08/29/how-to-create-a-positive-work-place-culture/.

Baumeister, Roy F., and Mark R. Leary. "The Need to Belong: Desire for Interpersonal Attachments as a Fundamental Human Motivation." *Psychological Bulletin,* 117, no. 3 (1995): 497–529. https://psycnet.apa.org/doi/10.1037/0033-2909.117.3.497.

Berger, David H. *Commandant's Planning Guidance: 38th Commandant of the Marine Corps*. Washington D.C.: Headquarters United States Marine Corps, 2019.

Bushman, Brad J. "Does Venting Anger Feed or Extinguish the Flame? Catharsis, Rumination, Distraction, Anger and Aggressive Responding." *Personality and Social Psychology Bulletin* 28, no. 6 (2002): 724–731. https://psycnet.apa.org/doi/10.1177/014616720228900 2.

Businessolver. *The State of Workplace Empathy: Fifth Annual Study.* Executive Summary, Businessolver.com, Inc. 2020.

Collins, Jim, and Jerry Porras. *Built to Last: Successful Habits of Visionary Companies.* Harper Business, 1994.

Covey, Stephen R. *The 7 Habits of Highly Effective Families.* St. Martin's Press, 1997.

Eisenhower, Dwight D. "Dwight D. Eisenhower Presidential Library, Museum & Boyhood Home." National Archives. Accessed February 10, 2025. https://www.eisenhowerlibrary.gov/eisenhowers/quotes#Leadership.

Esser, Frank. "Stimulus-Response Model." *Donsbach, W. The International Encyclopedia of Communication* 4836–4840. 2008.

Franklin, Benjamin. *Advice to a young Tradesman, written by an old One.* Boston: Benjamin Mecom, 1748.

Harter, J. K., et al. (2024). "The Relationship Between Engagement at Work and Organizational Outcomes": Q12 Meta-Analysis: 11th Edition. Gallup.

Languages, Oxford. *Oxford English Dictionary.* Accessed December 13, 2024. https://www.oed.com/search/dictionary/?scope=Entries&q=character+flaw.

Leotti, Lauren A., Sheena S. Iyengar, and Kevin N. Ochsner. "Born to Choose: The Origins and Value of the Need for Control." *Trends in Cognitive Science* 14, no. 10 (October 2010): 457–463. doi: 10.1016/j.tics.2010.08.001.

Lilius, Jacoba M., et al. "Compassion Revealed." White Paper. University of Michigan, 2013.

Mattis, James M., and Bing West. *Call Sign Chaos: Learning to Lead.* Random House, 2019.

Mayer, John D. 2008. "Emotional Intelligence and Leadership." *Journal of Applied Psychology* 93, no. 2 234–241.

Meyer, Urban, and Wayne Coffey. *Above the Line: Lessons in Leadership and Life from a Championship Season*. Penguin Books, 2015.

Nadella, Satya, Greg Shaw, and Jill Tracie Nichols. *Hit Refresh: The Quest to Rediscover Microsoft's Soul and Imagine a Better Future for Everyone*. Harper Business, 2017.

Nadella, Satya. "The Moment That Forever Changed Our Lives." October 21, 2017. Accessed September 12, 2024. https://www.linkedin.com/pulse/moment-forever-changed-our-lives-satya-nadella/.

Page, Susan. *The Power of Business Process Improvement*. AMACOM, 2010.

Peck, Scott M. *Further Along the Road Less Traveled: The Unending Journey Toward Spiritual Growth*. New York City: Simon & Schuster, 1993.

Phillips, Donald T. *Lincoln on Leadership: Executive Strategies for Tough Times*. Warner Books, 1992.

Schultz, Howard. *Pour Your Heart Into It: How Starbucks Built a Company One Cup at a Time*. Hyperion, 1997.

The Google re:Work team. "Understand Team Effectiveness." Google. Accessed December 11, 2024. https://rework.withgoogle.com/en/guides/understanding-team-effectiveness.

Yahoo! Finance. *Microsoft Corporation (MSFT)*. Accessed September 13, 2024. https://finance.yahoo.com/quote/MSFT/history/?guccounter=1&guce_referrer=aHR0cHM6Ly93d3cuZ29vZ2xlLmNvbS8&guce_referrer_sig=AQAAAEO2d2r6uhLtLV-Oqy5BFo1cC2jOJZUq9q54jwC81F6srum8GzmKopg9qz8kqYekNMytRpA8NPbgxXELWt5BnTf94r2JBdmTaeGKY9XdmD0vtS-b3NcXNCgpg9fIJg4UNL.

MEET THE AUTHOR

Olaolu Ogunyemi is a loving husband, father, mentor, award-winning writer, and US Marine officer with a deep passion for working with children and developing leaders. Known for his infectious energy and creativity, Olaolu channels his personality into every aspect of his work. As the fifth of six children, he learned the value of storytelling early, inspiring him to write books that foster meaningful family connections and teach invaluable life lessons.

He is the author of the award-winning and Amazon bestselling children's book *Crow From the Shadow*, along with *Horace the Horsefly* and *Billy Dipper's Time to Shine*. His professional insights and creative work have been featured in numerous publications and platforms, including *Military Families Magazine* (where he published "Lessons from a Deployed Father" and was separately highlighted for his work), the YouVersion Bible App, the *Marine Corps Gazette*, the *Parenting Decolonized* podcast, and many more publications, podcasts, and media outlets.

Olaolu's writing and speaking style captivates audiences by combining entertaining storytelling with practical insights, encouraging families and leaders alike to embrace challenges and grow. When he isn't mentoring or writing, he enjoys playing music, exercising, traveling, and spending quality time with his wife and children.

Connect with him at Parent-Child-Connect.com.